Current issues in community work

A study by
The Community Work Group

Chairman:
Lord Boyle of Handsworth
Vice-Chairmen:
Professor George Wedell
Dame Eileen Younghusband, D.B.E., J.P.
The Calouste Gulbenkian Foundation

Routledge & Kegan Paul
London and Boston

First published 1973
by Routledge & Kegan Paul Ltd
Broadway House, 68–74 Carter Lane
London EC4V 5EL and
9 Park Street
Boston, Mass. 02108, U.S.A.
Reprinted 1975
Printed in Great Britain
by Redwood Burn Limited
Trowbridge and Esher
© The Calouste Gulbenkian Foundation,
Lisbon, 1973

ISBN 0 7100 7687 8 (c)
ISBN 0 7100 7688 6 (p)

Library of Congress Catalog Card no. 73-83073

Contents

Foreword

Dr José de Azeredo Perdigão

*Chairman, The Calouste Gulbenkian
Foundation, Lisbon*

The Community Work Group sprang from conferences held in early 1969 to discuss the Gulbenkian Report, *Community Work and Social Change*, published the previous December. This was the Foundation's response to a request to set up for three years a nationally representative group for the exchange of information and ideas about community work and to study some of its more interesting manifestations. The Group met for the first time in January 1970, with its effectiveness virtually assured some weeks earlier when the Right Honourable Lord Boyle of Handsworth accepted the Foundation's invitation to become its Chairman. It is gratifying that the Foundation's belief has been confirmed—during the life of the group—that the years ahead would see important new roles for community work in social planning and social policy, in social work and in education.

The Group held its final meeting in January this year. The present book brings together the results of the work of the sub-groups which, for most of the Group's three-year lifetime, studied particular issues in community work and looked forward to the need for permanent means to continue further exploration of the subject. The Foundation would like to thank Group members and others from outside the Group who have contributed lavishly of their time and knowledge to the book's compilation. My fellow Trustees and I owe a special debt of thanks to the Vice-Chairmen, Dame Eileen Younghusband and Professor George Wedell, for their many valuable contributions. We are particularly glad to pay tribute to Lord Boyle's leadership, which gave the Group coherence and direction, and inspired a high level of discussion at the plenary sessions. We also wish to thank the Principal and staff of the National Institute for Social Work Training for making available offices, library and meeting rooms and creating an atmosphere of friendliness for the Group and its staff.

The Foundation invited members to serve in their personal capacity and the views expressed in the following pages must not be taken as representative of the organisations with which members are connected. It is the Foundation's belief that the Group has served the function of maintaining momentum and relevance in the continuing discussion of community work, so providing a basis for further discussion and practical experiment in the years to come.

Preface

The Right Honourable Lord Boyle
of Handsworth

Chairman of the Community Work Group

The Community Work Group was made possible by the generous sponsorship of the Gulbenkian Foundation and more particularly by the unfailing support of the Deputy Director of the British branch, as well as the competence of the Group's secretariat. The present book, which is the result of many discussions, does not set out to be a unanimous document drafted by a single hand. I would wish to acknowledge especially the hard work of the chairmen of the five sub-groups and the working party—all of whom remain anonymous.

I had suggested at a plenary meeting that not only the content of the draft and specific recommendations, but also the 'tone' had to be right; and this applied especially to the chapter on community action. We did not want to weary our readers with long stretches of definition and semantic argument, but the concept of 'community action' surely meant something different from community work or community development. I could not help being reminded, whenever we returned to those discussions, of a typically biting review by E. P. Thompson in *New Society** of the Report by Lord Radcliffe on the constitution of Warwick University. No sensible person would wish to revive a specific controversy which has, happily, receded far into the background. But there was one passage in this review which seemed to me highly relevant to our work. Lord Radcliffe had remarked of one particular issue that 'it was neither here nor there'— to which Thompson had replied that the Report taken as a whole had left no doubt as to who was 'here' and who was 'there'.

Now this was a challenge which we could not ourselves evade, and least of all in the chapter on community action. There were, notionally, three ways we could meet it. First, the tone of our discussion could imply—perhaps it would be better to say complacently accept —that our Group was basically 'here', and that community work should be developed by trained professionals for the sake of those who were 'there'. I was clear, myself, that such an approach would leave us open to devastating criticism. It would show that we had simply failed to give our minds to the meaning of 'community action',

* 'Report on Lord Radcliffe', *New Society*, no. 396, 30 April 1970, pp. 737–8.

or to listen to members of the Group who pointed out that it was hard to reconcile the role of community activist with that of a member of a profession. 'An important element of community action', one member reminded us, 'is to develop means by which the previous non-experts have greater influence; the emphasis is on reducing differences between persons, not maintaining them.'

A second way of meeting the 'here' and 'there' challenge was for us to attempt to sound as if the Group as a whole were 'there'. But I did not believe this would ring true—though it should be emphasised that certain individual members of the Group identified themselves as close to that position.

There was, however, a third possibility, namely that we should aim to persuade the decision-makers and the professionals to move with greater understanding towards the viewpoint of those who are 'there', and to attain a firmer grasp of their needs, not just for resources, but for structures with which they can feel genuinely identified. This is the approach we have adopted in the chapter on community action, where we have given detailed consideration both to the emergence of community action and to its main features. This chapter aroused considerable discussion in the Group. In the light of this discussion and of members' written comments, two members of the sub-group and I carried out a fresh revision of the draft.

I am sure that the concept of 'involvement' is crucial if we want to understand what community action is about; indeed it is precisely the desire to become more involved—to achieve a greater sense of place—that one quite frequently hears expressed by the constructively-minded leaders of minority racial groups. What about the implied questioning of 'professionalism' and the dangers of fostering too much of a client relationship? I have myself said often enough, in one context or another, that our society needs to set a higher value on the quality of professional performance, and no one can work in a university without becoming more aware of the part universities (along with other organisations) play in validating standards of professional competence which we all take for granted. And yet, however much one respects the professions, which must of their very nature emphasise the differences between practitioners and clients, there is surely an important place within our society for those activists who wish explicitly to challenge generally accepted values, and the criteria whereby resources are distributed. In a big city, when it comes to the administration of social and educational policies, there is a need for the highest standards of professional experience allied to creative imagination; I would suggest that there is also a special contribution to be made by rogue elephants who don't fit easily within the accepted institutional framework, yet possess the secret of gaining the confidence of those seeking to become more involved.

I hope that this book will be widely read by all those with a concern for the vitality of community life and for community work as an important means to this end. It is addressed to political leaders, senior officials in central and local government, social planners and administrators, those engaged full-time or part-time in the practice and teaching of community work, and members of other professions whose duties involve an understanding of community needs and ways of meeting them. Above all, it is addressed to the growing number of citizens who, out of personal concern, involve themselves voluntarily in community work aimed at a better society, both locally and in the country at large.

Some of the issues with which community work has to deal are echoed in the 'Living Voices' of people who are involved in their resolution. To them this book is dedicated.

Heard in a 'redevelopment area' in South London
If only we knew what was happening to us; they could come and tell us, don't you think.

Borough council alderman
We represent the people and I don't think it is up to us to ask them what they want.

Leader of a local group
To stick your neck out where you live takes real guts.

Local resident
The grass roots have woken up and they won't ever go to sleep again.

1 Introduction

The Group

The Community Work Group, consisting of some fifty-five members, was set up by the Calouste Gulbenkian Foundation for three years from the beginning of 1970, under the chairmanship of Lord Boyle of Handsworth. Members were invited to join the Group as individuals in a personal capacity and not as representatives. They included practising community workers, academics, civil servants and senior staff of local authorities, voluntary organisations and foundations. A list of members appears on pp. 145–8.

Background to its formation

Community Work and Social Change, the report of a much smaller Study Group on training also set up by the Foundation, was published late in 1968. Its findings were discussed at a series of regional conferences. At more than one of these, members urged that the momentum of interest generated by the original Study Group and its report should be maintained through a national forum for the further discussion of important issues in community work and that this forum should consist of people from diverse fields who would not otherwise meet and have opportunities for regular exchange of views.

Second, major social and structural changes had been proposed by the Kilbrandon (1964), Seebohm (1968), Redcliffe-Maud (1969) and Skeffington (1969) reports and in *Youth and Community Work in the 70s* (Youth Service Development Council, 1969); the Government had established the Educational Priority Areas (Plowden, 1967), the Urban Aid Programme and the Community Development Project;* pressure for participation by the community in planning and decision-making was increasing; and one of the five priorities adopted by the National Council of Social Service (1969) after a review of its work was to encourage citizen involvement in voluntary social action. Moreover the volume and variety of community work and the number of appointments made for its practice were increasing rapidly, together with the demand for wider opportunities for training.

* Initiated by the Home Office in 1969 in twelve selected areas.

At the same time, uncertainty and doubt persisted about the meaning and function of community work and its proper place, both in training and practice. The Gulbenkian Foundation decided that, in this climate of change, it would be desirable to stimulate further exchanges of view between leading personalities concerned with community work, as an influence towards clarification, co-ordination and integration of effort at this formative stage in its development.

Objects

Briefly stated, the aims of the Group have been, first to collect and exchange information and ideas about community work; and second to study particular aspects of the subject and to report results. It was clear from the outset that any attempt to study *all* aspects—when members' time and energies were heavily committed in their own fields—would be likely to lead the Group into diffuse and unprofitable deliberations. It was accordingly decided to concentrate on what members considered to be some of the cardinal issues in community work at the present time.

Method of working

The whole Group devoted ten meetings to the first object, collection and exchange of information. At each meeting, a major issue of topical importance to community work was discussed, on the basis of papers written by individual members. The value of these meetings turned less on the quality of the papers and the discussion than on the fact that people with very different roles, functions and interests in community work—senior civil servants, local authority planners, community workers practising in areas of social deprivation, and many others—did some of their thinking aloud in the presence of the others. This process was the Group's main *raison d'être* and it is arguable that in the event its most significant contribution was made through these meetings. It is important to establish the point, since the present report is not concerned with this part of the work of the Group.

Much time was given to the second object, the study of particular aspects of community work, of which this account is the result. At its second meeting in July 1970 the Group decided to divide into five sub-groups* (each consisting of some ten members) and to discuss and provide reports on the following topics:

  i.   methods and techniques in community work (later expanded to include also its varieties, assumptions and scope);
 ii.   community action;
iii.   the analysis of community projects;

* Not all members did in fact join a sub-group.

iv. the position and problems of community workers in statutory and voluntary services; and
v. training.

The sub-groups held a series of meetings between November 1970 and July 1972; from time to time, specialists were invited to join particular sub-groups' discussions and written material was also collected from various sources.

Early in 1972 each sub-group agreed on a synopsis for its report. The reports themselves were then drafted, amended after discussion at sub-group meetings and considered in July by an editorial committee appointed by the Group, consisting of the five chairmen of sub-groups. These reports thus became the six chapters which follow. The whole document except the last two chapters was then discussed by the Group at its plenary meeting in September. Meanwhile the Group had appointed ten of its members in May as a working party to consider the present needs in community work, national or local, and how these should be met. Its report, which forms the subject of chapter 8, was considered, and the document finally revised, by the end of January 1973 when the Community Work Group held its final meeting.

It has not been the aim or intention to resolve conflict or controversy or to secure agreement, either within or between sub-groups. Consistency has not been sought in the present study. On the contrary the aim has been to present conflicting points of view on unresolved issues. Consequently every member of the Group does not necessarily subscribe to the whole of the contents of this document. This is particularly relevant to chapter 4 on community action, which is the most controversial part of what follows.

The earlier study group report and certain general considerations

Since the Community Work Group may be said to have grown out of the Study Group of 1966–8, the report of the latter, *Community Work and Social Change*, has been taken as a starting point and no attempt is made below to cover the ground again. That report considered the significance of the word 'community' and quoted the following as covering some of the essential aspects succinctly (Gulbenkian Foundation, 1968, pp. 2, 3):

The *essence* of community is a sense of common bond, the sharing of an identity, membership in a group holding some things, physical or spiritual, in common esteem, coupled with the acknowledgement of rights and obligations with reference to all others so identified. We may designate several types of community. A *residence community* (also called an ecological community) is one in which the bond which unites the members is common

habitation of socially delineated physical space . . . The term
moral or psychic community is applied to those in which the
sense of membership rests on a spiritual bond involving values,
origins or belief. Either type may be largely *latent*, having
merely a potential for common action, or *active*, with members
interacting regularly and intensely. (From Inkeles, 1966, p. 69,
italics in original.)

It is noteworthy as an example of the difficulties of definition that
members of one sub-group, considering this in 1972, were unable to
agree on whether 'community', in its commonly accepted usage,
necessarily had, or had not, an exclusively geographical connotation.

The study group report characterised the nature and purpose of
community work as follows (Gulbenkian Foundation, 1968, pp. 3,
4, 5):

It typically consists of work with groups of local people who
have come into existence because they want to change something or
do something that concerns them. Community work also embraces
attempts to relate the activities of social agencies more closely
to the needs of the people they serve. This may include inter-agency
co-operation, study and planning, as well as similar action over
wider geographical areas or aspects of social policy . . .

Community work is essentially concerned with affecting the
course of social change through the two processes of analysing
social situations and forming relationships with different
groups to bring about some desirable change. It has three
main aims; the first is the democratic process of involving
people in thinking, deciding, planning and playing an active
part in the development and operation of services that affect
their daily lives; the second relates to the value for personal
fulfilment of belonging in a community; the third is concerned
with the need in community planning to think of actual people
in relation to other people and the satisfaction of their needs
as persons, rather than to focus attention upon a series of
separate needs and problems. This means working within constant
tensions between people's needs and the scarce resources
available to meet them, between the conflicting demands of
different groups, and different ideas about the kind of change
that is desirable. Organisational structures and administration
are also important in impeding or facilitating these purposes.

Community work is only one aspect of the far broader issue
of how to meet people's needs and give them an effective say in
what these are and how they want them met. It is part of a
protest against apathy and complacency and against distant
and anonymous authority. It is also part of the whole dilemma of
how to reconcile the 'revolution of human dissent' with the

large-scale organisation and economic and social planning which seem to be inseparably interwoven with the parallel revolution of rising expectations. This boils down to the problem of how to give meaning to democracy. Obviously many people are trying to do this in many ways. The question for community work is whether organisational structures can be devised and people trained and employed to facilitate citizen participation and to make it more effective, as well as making public and voluntary services more acceptable and usable. In short, community work is a means of giving life to local democracy.

Community work is further described in that report (p. 35) as having three 'strands':

Direct work with local people
Agency or inter-agency activities
Analysis, forecasting and planning.

These functions or aspects are often interwoven and could perhaps be more succinctly expressed as—

community (field) work
community organisation
community planning.

Within these broad descriptions, the boundaries of community work are necessarily arbitrary, if the term is not to be used in a nebulous, all-embracing fashion, in the sense in which everyone is regarded, in any social activity, as doing community work or engaged in community action. For instance, the sub-group which considered community action decided not to discuss this in relation to industry, employment or student activities within universities. Adult education, social work and youth work in particular are closely related to community work. There is some discussion of these relationships in this study, but we do not consider it feasible or desirable at present to attempt more precisely to delineate boundaries. It is more important to discover the essential core of an activity than to engage in demarcation disputes.

The relevance and potential of community work in particular settings is frequently over- or under-estimated by employing authorities. Community work is no more a panacea for the ills of society now than psychiatry was some years ago: community workers are, unfortunately, not magicians. Trained community workers are needed but equally important is an attitude of mind among other professionals and throughout society which might be described as 'community-oriented'. One of the tasks of the community worker is to encourage employing authorities (both official and voluntary), elected members and employees alike to be more concerned about community needs and aspirations. The Group endorsed the view of the earlier report that this attitude should be an integral element—not an afterthought or a bow towards the latest fashion—in orientation and training for other professions and for politicians.

The concept of community, whether geographically associated or not, is as much about people's *feeling* of common interest with others as about more tangible factors. A community-oriented attitude of mind may for example develop initially from within the neighbourhood, parochial or other local organisational level or through outside concern with the needs of decaying and deprived inner city areas. Such an attitude—and the growth of interest in community work itself—has recently been stimulated on the one hand by feelings of frustration at the scale, complexity and remoteness of modern social systems or power structures; and on the other hand by a more general desire or demand for participation, due in part to the development of social education, the increased mobility of population and the multiplying effect of the mass media of communication. An attitude of mind which ensures that needs, difficulties or problems and their solutions are always looked at from the standpoint of a local community and its members, as well as administratively or politically from above downwards, is likely, if widely diffused among men and women, to be a powerful agent of social change. This concept is developed more fully in chapter 3.

Whether community work is, or should be, a distinct professional activity, as well as an element in the training and practice of a wide range of occupations which minister to social needs or impinge on the life of the community, is a question discussed in the course of what follows. Suffice it to say here that if the full-time trained community worker is to fulfil an effective role in detecting needs, gaps or opportunities in community provision and in stimulating members of the community to work for fuller provision in co-operation with other professions, then he needs both standing and support.

The field of community work is now in process of rapid transformation and development. Some of the major policy documents and new enterprises have already been mentioned above. It may be useful to refer here to a number of others which contribute to the pace of change.

At least six departments in Whitehall are concerned: those in the charge of the Secretaries of State for Education and Science, for the Environment, for the Home Department, for Scotland, for the Social Services and for Wales. The Social Work (Scotland) Act 1968 and the Local Authority Social Services Act 1970 have established integrated social services throughout local government; and this integration is reflected, for practitioners, in the amalgamation which formed the British Association of Social Workers in 1970. The White Paper on the Redcliffe-Maud proposals (Department of Local

Government, 1970) inaugurated a radical structural change; while the Green Paper on the National Health Service (Department of Health and Social Security, 1970) has lately been followed by proposals for reorganisation (Department of Health and Social Security, 1972). The Aves report (1969) is a mark of the importance attached to encouraging members of the community to volunteer for social service. Decisions have also been taken on the recommendations in the Skeffington report on participation in planning (Department of the Environment, 1972). The Russell and Alexander Committees on Adult Education* are about to publish their findings.

At the same time, many local authorities, new town corporations, councils of social service and other organisations are employing community workers in a variety of settings and stimulating or supporting many community projects. The Community Relations Commission, set up under the Race Relations Act of 1968, is actively concerned with cognate problems.

In the voluntary field, councils of social service throughout the country have tended to alter the direction of their effort from promoting particular projects towards encouraging community councils or residents' groups, through which the local community may identify its needs and decide in what order of priority these should be met—a change towards a community development and away from a paternalistic role. A growing number and variety of other independent bodies, whether operational, financing or research organisations, are actively engaged in encouraging community work or in training or study. The Association of Community Workers has, since 1968, offered a forum for those working in this field and has now (1973) decided on a broader basis for membership, with less emphasis on qualifications or experience.

Moreover, it should not be assumed that the barometer is set for change because of action 'from above'; indeed many of these developments are in fact responses to community pressure. There has been a tremendous growth in spontaneous community action and pressure groups—tenants' associations, claimants' unions, squatter movements, citizens' rights organisations and others.

Local communities now protest more frequently in strength against changes made without consultation or insist, if necessary by demonstration, on local or central authorities hearing their grievances or allegations of neglect or indifference. Increasingly, such protest is directed against the effects on local communities of the socially arbitrary decisions of big businesses or nationalised industry, for instance in re-location or technological development. The democratic right to protest and to be heard and answered by those in power has a very long history in this country; but its recent exercise has become

* Terms of reference quoted on p. 117. Russell Committee Report published March 1973.

more widespread, more emphatic and often more effective. Community groups have been making it clear that they can and will hold authority directly to account and expect a proper hearing and a reasoned response.

In this climate of rapid change, a greater or lesser degree of conflict is inevitable and often healthy. We have frequently discussed conflict and its value; but have not reached any conclusion on its limits. We hope that a reasoned discussion of some of the critical issues in this field may contribute towards an understanding of the potential of community work and of the role of community workers in developing and improving the quality of life of individual people in society. We hope also that what follows will be read and debated, in particular by practitioners in all those professions which serve the community, by leaders of community groups and by officials and elected members in both central and local authorities, corporations and other social systems. We do not presume to have clarified the issues discussed in any definitive sense but hope that we have succeeded in stimulating further thought and continuing dialogue.

NOTE
The Community Work Group ceased to exist at the end of January 1973. A few subsequent developments are referred to in footnotes.

2 The scope and values of community work

The upsurge of interest

A discussion of community work in Britain in the 1970s must take note of its diversity and its dynamic growth. The word 'community', elusive and vague though its meanings may be, has become fashionable and many practical efforts are being made towards the promotion of what is called 'community work' in a large number of fields. There are many explanations for this conscious attention to features of social and political life which earlier generations had taken for granted. The most fundamental explanation is concerned with values, a sense that all is not well with our society with its tendency towards large-scale, impersonal administrations, towards technological and materialistic goals and towards a subordination of the individual by what is often called 'the system'. The rate of change to which social systems or structures and individuals have to respond interrupts stable relationships and calls for constant adaptation to new patterns of organisation and to larger bureaucratic systems, which exist to serve the personal needs of people, yet seem remote from them. There is a desire to assert the role of the individual in his ability to participate, to share in the decisions that affect his way of living and to take a more active part in his society. The term 'democratic' is often used to describe these aims and processes: a democracy which includes a network of new groupings added to the traditional, representative political institutions, so as to give each person the greatest possible opportunity for taking part.

One of the commonly stated assumptions about community work is that it is a natural growth, taking root slowly as people live and work together. Outside intervention is neither desirable nor is it usually successful. This assumption is based on the traditional idea of community as an element in locality or neighbourhood. But owing to the nature of modern, urban society with its high mobility, its mixed populations, the decline of unifying institutions such as the churches and the lack of opportunities for potential leaders to emerge, it seems increasingly difficult for members of a community to become actively involved in local affairs, whether we think of a situation in a

9

depressed area or new town or in a rural setting. Indeed the increasing incidence and effect of social mobility may provide the most obvious justification for the community worker's intervention. Experience suggests that people are more likely to find their associations through interest groups which may cover a wide geographical area. They need institutions to which they can belong. They need leaders who have the time and the skills to develop these institutions and to find out what people want. It is because so many areas of the country lack social opportunities and people lead isolated, lonely and sometimes empty lives, that full-time community workers with training and experience are being increasingly employed. In new towns they have proved their value as they have in some of the housing estates of Greater London and elsewhere (see Central Housing Advisory Committee, 1967; Goetschius, 1969).

Part of the upsurge of interest is practical. As life becomes more complex, it is as difficult for the administrator as for the citizen to escape from the fragmentation imposed by specialised technology. The rapidity of social change accentuates the dangers to the common good which arise from sectional approaches. The need for consulta- tion and planning to take account of the citizen's general interests is widely recognised and the people, it is claimed, have a positive role to play in the shaping of policies at all levels which affect their lives and those of their children. Citizens' rights groups, consumer groups, tenants' associations or shop floor groups are a few examples of community efforts through which people seek to secure more control over their lives. Social planning, urban aid programmes, community relations councils and community development projects are examples of government interest.

Yet another explanation for the growth of community work is the recognition by existing workers that community work methods can contribute to more effective work; it may be essential to improve specific or general aspects of a neighbourhood by inviting community participation from those who live in and know the area. Social work, following the Seebohm and Kilbrandon reports, is actively exploring how to develop the new methods. Those engaged in adult education and youth work are also experimenting widely with non-institutional approaches and with more informal styles of work. Planners too are seeking effective ways of increasing participation in planning. Voluntary groups are attempting increasingly to co-ordinate their efforts and to plan future activities in co-operation with the people as well as with the statutory bodies. Similarly it is the aim of many church and religious groups to promote community work in areas of social need. The increasing recognition by the government of the contribution made by volunteers is another example of a changing emphasis towards involving members of the community. Some of this community work is an end in itself, seeking to develop and extend people's capacity for social relationships and their social skills. Some of it attempts to mobilise community effort to improve the environment or specific services and falls within the long tradition of voluntary social innovation and reform. There is also evidence of growth in the number of spontaneous self-help and community action groups and of co-operation among voluntary agencies.

Varieties of community work

There are, as has been suggested, many different reasons for the growing interest which has arisen in various quarters. Community work as an instrument has wide application throughout society but there is a special need for its application, with adequate resources, in areas where seriously socially deprived people are living. The result is a wide range of philosophy, objectives and methods which makes definition and classification extremely difficult. It is clear that many activities are labelled community work when people are involved in seeking common aims or purposes; these may cover a great variety of objectives. Other activities which use the initiative and participation of members to promote social action may or may not be regarded as community work. The Study Group in its report, *Community Work and Social Change*, made an analysis of the scope and methods of community work, which includes three main levels of work and emphasises the differences in methods between those that are non-directive and those that involve more precise preconceived aims (Gulbenkian Foundation, 1968, chapters 3 and 6). The levels of work are:

The 'grass roots' or neighbourhood level: settlements, community centres, social and educational work in housing estates or in the older centres of cities are familiar examples. More recent examples, sponsored by government in co-operation with particular local authorities, are the Community Development Project and the Educational Priority Areas. The objectives of the Community Development Project are to find out, through experiments in social action, how to effect a lasting improvement in social situations in which individuals, families and communities cannot function adequately, by studying needs and aspirations in such neighbourhoods, and helping the services provided by local and central government, in the light of the study, to respond to needs, to promote community involvement and development and to contribute towards effective social planning. Educational Priority Areas, a term devised by the Central Advisory Council for Education (England) (1967) in the Plowden report, are most commonly found in the inner regions of large cities. They are characterised by all or most of the following conditions: poverty, resulting from unemployment and very low wages associated with unskilled work; obsolete and overcrowded housing; a depressing physical environment; and a concentration of immigrant households. Among the consequences of these conditions for schools are low levels of educational expectation and attainment; a high turnover of pupils and teachers; and truancy and early leaving from secondary schools. Action research projects financed by the Department of Education and Science and the Social Science Research Council have been mounted in a number of these areas (in Birmingham, Liverpool, London and the West Riding; see Halsey, 1972). But there are many other local authority and voluntary experiments providing ways of involving members of a local community, such as work with the unattached, with drug addicts, with single-parent families and with other groups which are isolated, lonely or deprived;

The local agency and inter-agency level: community work here is more formally organised, e.g. in establishing and sustaining a secondary group such as an old people's welfare council, a women's, a youth or an arts council, to represent and to service other 'grass roots' groups. The task is one of co-ordinating local groups vertically with district groups, with wider city or regional groups and from there with a national organisation; or the co-ordination may be horizontal, notably as in councils of social service and in federations of youth or women's organisations, bringing together different bodies with common interests. This administrative and institutional type of community work is characteristic both of voluntary and statutory bodies and needs to go on at the neighbourhood level, as well as at the district or town level. The degree to which a worker participates in decision-making and in activity varies greatly. The mutual aid organisation may have a stronger democratic constitution than the philanthropic or the statutory body;

The level of regional or national community planning: this is less focused on day-to-day or specific programmes and more concerned with future developments and policy, taking a number of interrelated aspects into account. The interest in the environment, in new towns and overspill projects, in development areas, in the regeneration of the decaying inner centres of cities, are examples of comprehensive planning which have a direct bearing on the patterns and quality of life of large numbers of people. The Skeffington report (*People and Planning*, 1969) raised some of the issues of how to reconcile the objectives of the physical planners with the social and personal well-being of the people affected by the plan.

In practice the interrelation between these three levels of community work is continuous. The leaders of the local group must present their case to and negotiate with local authorities and other organisations for services and resources. The group may properly make proposals for change and action in this way and may in turn be consulted by the planners. The mass media may play a significant role in furthering or confusing the issues. While most people recognise that the vitality of community work depends on the vigour of the 'grass roots' groups, these are the ones which tend to be neglected both by the formally organised bodies and by the planners; a conscious effort is needed to make and keep open channels of communication between them. Methods in community work reflect in some degree the different levels of work and the functions they serve. At the ends of a continuum are:

non-directive methods where decision and action lies with the members of the group themselves. The characteristics are self-determination, a process where the group identifies its own needs, makes its own plans and works largely by self-help to their realisation. The community worker is an enabler in this process, not the director or manager (Batten, 1967);

directive methods where the main decisions are taken by the official or leader or council and programmes and policies are worked out on this basis. Imposition rather than self-determination is the characteristic and active participation may be limited to a small committee or inner official group. The principle is to work *for* the community rather than *with* them.

In a real situation the sharp distinction between a fully democratic method and a strongly authoritarian or paternalistic method is not clear cut. In the different stages of development within programmes, directive or non-directive methods may be used according to the professional judgment of the worker and the nature of his responsibility. Operationally, a wide range of methods may be used and although these may vary from non-directive to highly task-oriented, the given objectives may be served by either, and by other methods or by a combination of methods, since community work is not merely a process but aims to achieve a stated goal. The larger the scale of organisation, however, the more complex its parts and the more technical the decisions which have to be made, the more difficult becomes direct involvement of ordinary people in decisions and in active participation of all kinds. Thus there may be a necessity to differentiate between the consultation stage and the final decision-making stage.

Patterns of community work

Various patterns of community work may be distinguished among the current forms of practice in a fluid scene. We suggest these four separate categories in order to illustrate the difficulties of adequate definition or classification:

1   *Focused on types of practice and employment*

Community work as a method of social work practised in the social services—

> preventive (as in areas of high social risk, or with vulnerable groups);
>
> supportive (as in group work with single-parent families, ex-prisoners or drug addicts);
>
> community self-help (as in promotion of children's playgroups, or the use of volunteer services).

Community work as a method in education practised in educational settings—

> establishment of social or recreational groups (social clubs, drama or sports groups);
>
> promotion of knowledge about current issues by discussion group or project methods (adult education, community work in schools and the development of the community school concept);
>
> work to increase participation in a variety of voluntary and statutory bodies (youth enterprise, civic societies, work groups).

Community work as a method in administration and policy-setting—

> creation of social action groups to find new opportunities or to fight for rights; also action research and development programmes;
>
> organisation of machinery for co-ordination of services both between agencies (horizontal: councils of social service) and within services (vertical: national and federated bodies with affiliated local groups);
>
> establishment of political machinery to give direct participation to local groups in community life, e.g. parish councils, citizen forums, community councils, civil liberties groups.

Development of social planning groups with wide responsibility for informing and consulting the public—

> replanning of decayed inner city areas involving demolition and rehousing (Liverpool, Tower Hamlets etc.);
>
> social development in new towns, large housing estates or overspill projects (see Central Housing Advisory Committee, 1967);
>
> regional planning in areas of social need (Scottish Highlands and Islands Development Board, Clydebank);

concentration of resources and study in selected neighbourhoods (Government Community Development Project, Educational Priority Areas).

2 *Focused on objectives*

Radical activism which questions the existing basis of society and proposes alternatives. The range here is considerable, from religious communes, through groups seeking alternative ways of living and working to power-seeking or anarchist groups. The groups may aim to promote a way of life of their own or to find a means of changing the existing structure of society. Issues about power and resources are critical. Conflict or confrontation may be a characteristic of such groups.

Development of the democratic process through more effective communication, participation and sharing of decision within the present administrative and economic system. The variety here is enormous in the methods used and the degree to which authority is effectively shared between the administration and the people. The principle of consensus based on reasoned discussion and compromise is usually assumed in these attempts to make institutions more democratic and more responsive to people's desires and needs.

The achievement of specific reforms through community action by pressure groups and consumer organisations such as the Child Poverty Action Group, claimants' unions, tenants' associations and a host of others.

Promotion of community groups as a means to enrich the life of members by fellowship, self-help and community service.

In some of these objectives community groups are regarded as an end in themselves, in others as a means to wider ends, some of which may be political or aimed at improving the quality of life. Both types depend on active leadership.

3 *Focused on the worker*

Community work in a range of professional and administrative tasks, e.g. among architects and planners; medical officers of health; directors of social services; housing managers or educational administrators; industrial managers;

community work as a part of political, trade union or religious leadership;

community work as a voluntary activity in countless organisations;

community work as a full-time, paid job in voluntary or statutory organisations and in informal groups.

Focused on theory

Political philosophy and theory as a justification for intervention and as a statement of objective. The maximum participation, self-determination and consensus approach represents one position. The radical, activist, conflict approach represents another.

Organisation, systems and management theories as explanations and guidelines for administrative tasks;

Sociological theories to provide understanding of social structure and social change and to give some grasp of social research findings and methods;

Group dynamics as a framework for the construction of inter-personal and inter-group process (see Bion, 1961; Batten, 1967).

In training, these and other theoretical orientations are usually taught at middle level. A practice theory which brings them together in a significant way is not yet developed.

These attempts to classify the many reasons for the current interest in community work and the variety of its methods, settings and objectives suggest the danger of any single or narrow definition. It is perhaps healthy in a dynamic society that there should be many strands of philosophy and of experiment, and this diversity is not unique to Britain (see Dunham, 1970 for the USA). The United Nations has recently (1971) been examining its twenty years of support for community work.

Values

The assumptions underlying community work are essentially statements of values and these are very differently understood and expressed by different groups in our society. Perhaps at the most basic level of generality three propositions are fairly widely agreed:

The first of these is that people matter and that policies, administrative systems and organisational practices should be judged by their effect on people: whether they contribute to the ability of people to lead satisfying lives and to minimising deprivation and drop-out by those who have difficulty in surviving. Society is made up of complex networks and the conflicts and harmony between the networks determine in large measure the quality of life. To state this is to emphasise a dynamic and ultimately an ethical view of society as against a purely materialistic or technological view. Community work is concerned to give practical expression, in a great many different ways, to a philosophy that puts people at the centre of things.

The second proposition is that people acting together develop their capacities as human beings. A society should give the maximum opportunity for the active participation of people in every aspect of the environment, social, economic and political. The importance of this principle today lies in the degree to which the scale and complexity of modern society has made the direct involvement of people difficult, and often apparently impossible. To the basic ideas about a political democracy have been added ideas about shared knowledge and decision in many other spheres of life—in industry and commerce, in the social services, in physical planning and leisure pursuits, to mention only a few. The relationship between people and bureaucracies is a central part of the discussion and further reference is made to this in chapter 3.

The third assumption relates to the sharing and redistribution of power in any given society or community in pursuit of the search for greater social equality and social justice. A concern with distribution of resources, benefits, power and influence follows inevitably from social surveys which identify groups with needs that are not being met in the current ordering of society's resources; and from the experience, through working with people rather than for them, of geographical areas and groups of people which are socially disadvantaged and excluded from exercising an influence over the management of social institutions which are provided for their benefit. Emphasis upon claimants' rights, upon conditions of living and upon the access of deprived people to the seats of power and decision-making is a natural and proper part of community work. This may legitimately lead to social action designed to enhance the status of such groups and their members' control over their own lives and ability to express their aspirations and concerns.

Once these propositions are stated, the debate about ends and means becomes vigorous and diverse. As has been said earlier, some community groups take the view that only by creating an alternative society or establishing self-contained communities, can the individual or social group be freed from the oppressions of 'the system'. There are deep political and religious issues involved in these attitudes.

Other community groups seek to improve the existing arrangements on their own initiative and the remarkable growth of pressure groups such as the Confederation for the Advancement of State Education, The National Association for the Welfare of Children in Hospital, claimants' unions, or the Disabled Income Group is evidence for this (see Jerman, 1971). The increase in the volunteer movements such as Task Force, the Young Volunteer Force and Youth Enterprise and the official encouragement of volunteers in hospitals, in the probation and after-care services and elsewhere is further evidence (Aves, 1969). Some schools now include community work as part of the curriculum. At the statutory level community work is becoming a part of the new social services or social work departments as it has long been a part of the work in new towns and in some housing and education departments. In deprived areas, as has been said, the Home Office has sponsored a series of community development projects. Some community-type activities qualify for urban aid. The Community Relations Commission is government-supported in its work in ethnically mixed areas. In the proposals to reorganise local government there has been much discussion about the creation of a small neighbourhood, parish or ward unit within the political and administrative set-up, and of community councils in Scotland.

The assumptions about the nature of community work practice are not always clear. On the one hand, as for example with pressure groups, community work is a means to some other end (i.e. task-centred) which may be the achievement of a safer street crossing, a playground or a local clinic. The improvement of services and of the environment creates innumerable opportunities for community action, sometimes in a short-term burst and in other cases, as with the preservation of the countryside, in long-term movements involving many groups in a sustained activity toward social development. Work with the elderly, the handicapped, single-parent families and other such groups provide further examples. On the other hand, community work may be seen as an end in itself (i.e. process-oriented), as means to create fellowship and a more satisfying life through people coming together in social, recreational or other activities. The term *project* has often been used to describe a community task which aims to establish a new service or to do battle with some arbitrary authority. The term *process* implies sharing and working together to develop knowledge and confidence and good social relationships.

To sum up, while there is enormous variety in the goals of community work, three main purposes may be identified:

the achievement of a task or tasks,
the establishment of good social relationships, and
the development of better capacity to cope with the complexities
or stresses of life,
or a combination of these.

In pursuit of goals or purposes, some of the more difficult assumptions about community work relate to concepts of authority, power and the distribution of resources. The issues are both philosophical and practical. In what ways can community work give individuals and groups a real say in the running of affairs in a world of complex and large scale organisations with vast technical resources? (See Marris and Rein, 1967.) What values do we attach and in what contexts to efficiency, to speed of decision, to rational and impartial administrative procedures (Weber, 1964) and what values to human qualities, to diversity and to personal initiative? This is an old debate on the principles it raises, but a modern debate in the context of a very mobile and dynamic industrial society. Community work is at the heart of this debate. Many of the activist groups reflect a will not only to protest but to change the distribution of power and for some, conflict, confrontation and even violence become to them legitimate means to the ends they seek (Alinsky, 1969).

Social action, however, is more widely if less spectacularly represented by a vast number of social groups which seek to redress the balance of power by working for specific reforms on behalf of their members. The Pre-School Playgroups Association and the Nursery Schools Association are interesting examples. Housing and rents provide a host of illustrations ranging from the squatters' and Shelter movements to local tenants' associations, rent protests, or self-help housing groups. There are few fields in national life where there are not active groups working to secure new services or resources or to improve those that exist. The community worker, voluntary or full-time, is often described as the communication link between the group he serves and those who have the resources and the power to decide on their allocation. It is a measure of the extent to which power and resources lie with large organisations that so much of community work has the characteristic of social action. The remedy sought may be a specific need or a redress of social injustice.

It is well known that organisations once established develop a life of their own, not necessarily related to their declared purposes. The members of any organisation tend automatically to close ranks and fight off changes in structure or objectives which they may consider threaten its existence and so their habitual way of working or even their livelihood and life style. As a service organisation grows, so are its members liable to become less receptive to the human feelings and needs of those whom it exists to serve. There is a temptation to treat an office file as 'more real' than the people who 'pass through' its pages. These tendencies are a major obstacle to community work and contribute much to the present mood of disillusionment with representative democracy. To combat this defensive and negative feature of our society's structure is far from easy; we make one practical suggestion in chapter 3, p. 30.

A final point in this discussion about assumptions at a practical level is the role of community work within social work. The social work departments in Scotland and the social services departments in England and Wales are beginning to work towards a community orientation both in the wider involvement of the public in their programmes and policies and by the specific use of community workers within the professional teams. At the same time there has been a move within the unified departments (formed in 1968 and 1970 when the former children, welfare and the social work components of the health departments were brought together, with the probation service in Scotland) towards research, inquiry and fact-gathering, in

to quantify more accurately the data on which relevant new
pments should be planned.

Scope

Community work has tended to develop, in the main, with young
people in a variety of settings but increasingly with older people
affected by social change. In new towns in particular and in deprived
areas it has extended to a wider age range of people. The growing
awareness of the needs of the elderly, the handicapped and the
mentally ill, discharged prisoners or their families, young mothers,
widows or the addicted or other groups with identifiable needs raises
the question of the extension of community work to include these
groups. Traditionally they have been assisted by voluntary bodies but
are now increasingly helped through the statutory social services.
They all need specific supporting services to meet their special needs;
but they are also people who should form part of the wider community with a chance to take part in community activities and they
need help to manage their lives and their social relationships with
as much independence as possible. It is in this last aspect that
community work seems to have an increasingly important part to
play in enabling people to plan, organise and direct their own
activities towards ends which they value.

When people from a restricted age range or suffering from a similar
disability form a group, this may well aid mobility and offer com-
panionship and stimulus, but there is then a risk, if the group is
managed too paternally, that the members of it may not enjoy the
common feeling that comes from shared values, beliefs, interests and
purposes and may fail to communicate across the boundaries of age
or condition. In principle the whole community should be the concern
of the worker.

3 Community work methods

Methods in community work are diverse because the objectives, the types and the levels of community work are so varied. The advocate of radical social change may use methods aimed towards conflict and confrontation. The gradualist may use a method to secure the greatest possible level of agreement and of shared decision, what is often called the consensus method. Method derives both from a moral position and from the practical nature of the problem to be solved.

Basic methods

In general, certain basic methods are followed in most community work activities as a kind of six-step progression:

study the situation;

establish rapport, good relationships and a network of communication links with the community;

gather information, analyse the relationship between community wants and needs and identify alternative ways of meeting needs, so as to formulate objectives;

create some basis of organisation and of resources (money, buildings, equipment, personnel) to promote activity and action (the movement from an informal to a more formal basis);

work on the programme, modifying procedures and objectives as experience grows;

review and evaluate progress to determine the next steps.*

Methods in community work are in essence attempts to solve problems of many different kinds. It is necessary to face the dilemma of how to reconcile the interests of opposing groups and of several co-existent groups competing for scarce resources. The problems usually concern people and groups playing the parts both of activators

* For a fuller discussion of the stages of community work see Gulbenkian Foundation, 1968, pp. 65–76.

and of consumers. The quality of diagnostic thinking includes not just an assessment of facts but also judgments about behaviour and feelings. The consequences of action in the short term and the longer term are at issue and thus moral questions are raised in every act of intervention. The decision is not just what can be done and who should do it, but what ought to be done. And within this wider framework of thinking, which most community workers consider must involve the community itself, plans are made. Experience shows that in the consideration of ends and of means there is need for considerable flexibility. What originally may appear as the main problem and the best ways of solving it, can easily change as the perceptions of the worker and the group develop. Diagnostic thinking, whether at 'grass roots' level or at planning level, needs to reflect this dynamic and sometimes apparently unpredictable nature of community life and to respond to it.

Case studies of the different steps in problem-solving often show the degree to which the original objectives become displaced. They emphasise the interaction within and between the many groups involved in a community project and the influence of the worker or officials. Studies of methods of work rightly focus on these inter-actions and particularly on the critical role of the leader. The leader-ship role varies according to the personality of the leader and the method he uses, whether paternalistic or democratic. The role is constrained by the nature of the tasks he has to perform, the relation-ships he is able to establish with the group and those which form within the group. Some situations demand a specialised competence and knowledge or an ability for quick analysis and rapid decisions. Other situations, as in neighbourhood work, allow for a variety of approaches and the worker can leave the decision about what is done and how it is done largely to the people. But where apathy is strong or where there is a marked lack of social cohesion, the worker may initially at least decide to exercise a more dominant role. Methods of leadership vary widely according to the scale and complexity of the tasks. What is possible at the 'grass roots' becomes difficult in large organisations operating through formal committee machinery. At the planning level the whole process of consultation, of shared knowledge and decision demands a conscious and structured approach if there is to be real interaction between planners and people. These different styles of leadership and the methods they involve are beginning to be systematically studied by fieldworkers through the Association of Community Workers and action research teams. Most of the material remains in pamphlet form or as articles in journals.*

Attempts to clarify community work methods are also being made

* See for example *Community Work Journal*, OUP; School and Community Kits, Community Service Volunteers, Toynbee Hall, London E1.

in the increasing number of training courses in universities, colleges and polytechnics. Method largely results from systematic analysis of common factors at work in a range of particular tasks in practical situations. It also has its basis in the values which guide intervention in community work. It also makes use of theory derived from the social and political sciences. Methods are a combination of the empirical and pragmatic, the ideological and reformist and the application of theoretical knowledge. The community worker needs knowledge in many fields and pursues it through many methods. He needs an understanding of organisation theory as well as a knowledge of administrative tasks. He draws on the results of social research and must have some competence in making objective studies of social structures and social problems. Behavioural studies from psychology, sociology and anthropology provide a range of insights which not only suggest alternative explanations for social events but also help to correct impressionistic and stereotyped thinking. Training can help to develop qualities of objectivity and of self-awareness as well as a capacity for informed analysis. The complexity of community work in modern Britain makes training essential if methods of work are to rest on more than common sense and goodwill. The subject is explored further in chapter 7.

Techniques and skills

Thus the methods used in community work centre on particular kinds of problem-solving. To analyse the nature of the task from experience, descriptions of community work prepared by fieldwork members of the Community Work Group have been collated. These accounts of roles and functions clarify some of the skills and techniques which the task demands. But what follows does not refer to the contribution made to systematic knowledge of community work by the social and behavioural sciences, nor is it suggested that every community worker necessarily covers all the ground. The descriptions by community workers are analysed under three main headings:

the qualities needed by the worker,
the knowledge on which he draws, and
the different roles he undertakes in the course of his work.

The community work described in the papers includes: community relations in Northern Ireland; social development in a new town; youth enterprise in a midland city; a family advice centre; community relations in an ethnically mixed area; a youth and community association in Scotland; a neighbourhood project in London. The focus is on 'grass roots' work within a defined locality, although many of the projects serve a whole city and a large number and variety of groups.

Qualities required by a community worker

Ability to establish relationships, to communicate and to create confidence;

accessibility to all members of the community and to representatives of organisations across age, social and political barriers;

flexibility in adapting to many situations—the ability to 'wear many hats';

sensitivity and patience and ability to work at the pace of the group;

capacity to work towards long-term objectives.

Knowledge required in community work

Intimate knowledge of local social and political structures, local services, facilities and sources of support;

knowledge of processes of group interaction, methods of communication, educational methods;

Knowledge of organisation, e.g. procedures in committees, at public meetings, processes in referrals, office administration including finance;

Knowledge of programme development, the running of group activities and the management of premises.

The content of the job

Study of the community in all its aspects, using both statistical and factual information and the feelings of people in a continuous process of interaction;

reconnaissance and analysis, surveys, diagnosis, prognosis, review of progress and achievements;

problem-solving, helping a group to clarify issues, decision-making, adoption of a strategy, planning of tasks;

working as a member of a team, helping groups to form and to work towards their aims, understanding the roles of other workers and agencies;

co-operation with voluntary and statutory bodies and influential individuals and groups, acting as a link to provide information, advice, guidance and referral;

mediation between conflicting interests, personalities and groups;

administrative and secretarial work with and for groups, including minutes, records, accounting, fund-raising, negotiations with statutory bodies;

training indigenous leaders, on-the-job training for helpers, student supervision;

public relations, speaking, broadcasting, editing and publishing, press liaison conferences, exhibitions, campaigns, protest meetings;

working with uninvolved people in detached work or where membership and support is poor, recruitment of volunteers;

political involvement in advocacy in helping to meet community needs.

This analysis is illustrative, not exhaustive.

The workers' own views of their roles and functions, when presented in this shorthand form, suggest a bewildering multiplicity of tasks, often conflicting and thus demanding a considerable range of skill and knowledge, as well as personal qualities of objectivity and integrity. The summaries cannot give a coherent picture of what is actually done and how it is done. But many interesting points come out. One skill clearly lies in the worker's planning of time and priorities. Another skill is the ability to change roles to meet different situations, for example to conduct a formal discussion at the town hall or to make informal contacts with a street group; to act as secretary to a committee or to be the principal speaker at a public meeting. One important skill mentioned lies in enabling people to run their own organisation, giving support in time of difficulty and helping them to realise that they do in fact control the organisation. The capacity to know how deep should be the involvement in a particular project and when to withdraw emphasises the importance of clear diagnosis and evaluation as well as a high degree of self-awareness and self-discipline. Administrative skills come high on the list, but a special kind of administration where the worker is aware of his role as a communication link and enabler, as a source of information and contact, but not as a manager.

One report showed that the workers, serving some thirty community groups, spend their time on committee work, office work, negotiating with statutory authorities and support and advice to local groups. The same report suggested that the workers need more knowledge of the local community and its social and political structure, how groups interact and the grants and benefits available to the community. There was need for increased skill in various

educational techniques, the communication of ideas and the organisation and running of meetings and conferences.

The teamwork which community work demands involves a clear
appreciation of the different roles and functions of many kinds of
workers and agencies. It also demands a clear perception of the
worker's own role and how that role may be seen by others. There
are many difficulties in avoiding subjective perceptions about roles,
one's own and other people's, and a constant risk of confusing feelings
about job, status, personality as felt by the worker with what is
the actual role, namely what can be and what is done. The quality of
sensitivity, which summarised records of work emphasise, is of
special importance. Differing professional and agency roles are
however only one of the networks in which the community worker is
involved. His main tasks lie with the community groups with which
he works, in all their complexity and variety. He needs remarkable
sensitivity in his relationships with them. The conclusion emerges
that an important function in community work is that of being an
effective interpreter within and between these many groups, official
and voluntary, formal and informal, with a special responsibility
towards the deprived and the inarticulate.

Community work and society

There are many unresolved questions about assumptions, settings
and methods in community work, about its place in statutory or
voluntary services, about control of resources, about the limits of
pressure and action and about problem-solving processes; there is
also the broader consideration of the role of community work in a
democratic society. The introduction to the Gulbenkian study group
report of 1968 contains these challenging words: 'community work
is part of a protest against apathy and complacency and against
distant and anonymous authority . . . [it] is a means of giving life to
local democracy' (pp. 4–5). This could form a preface to a discussion
of participation by people in decision-making and of some of the
methods which could help towards re-interpreting democracy in a
technological age.

It is assumed in what follows that the institutions of society will
not become authoritarian; will remain founded upon the rule of law
and not upon arbitrary power. However lethargic, erratic, misdirected or indifferent may be the response of these institutions to
the specific wishes and needs of individuals or community groups,
they are themselves in essence democratic: the elected representatives
of the people take major decisions and are expected to control the
administration and public funds, both central and local; and each
voter has a say in a change of government, whether parliamentary
or local.

Democratic control and arbitrary power

Why state what everyone knows? The fundamental distinction both of principle and of style of life between democratic control and arbitrary state power does need to be constantly restated—not least in a discussion of community participation. The bureaucracy, whether in central government departments or in local authorities, is ultimately accountable to elected representatives but the extent to which it is actually controlled by them is subject to change and open to criticism. Through a network of political and other groups, through parliamentary questions and by other means, pressure can be, and is, constantly brought to bear on official action or inaction. The contrasting structure is one in which the executive power is self-appointed and in no degree accountable to the community.

This distinction is true in theory but in practice the response to community pressure often seems to get weaker, slower and more reluctant; human dignity and individual needs seem increasingly to be submerged in stereotyped forms and responses by computer. Protests and demonstrations are in part outbursts of indignation against this, whatever their specific aim. For attempts to discuss, consult or participate on the part of people outside 'the system' can be defeating, even humiliating. People are inclined to feel that they are being 'moved about like luggage' within the system and this apparent lack of respect for their feelings breeds a mounting resentment against 'the establishment'. Such strong emotions and feelings of hostility pose a threat to democracy because they block the mind; reason ceases to operate and rational argument does not convince. Increasingly, people resent a decision, not necessarily because they can offer a better solution but simply because their views have not been sought or heard.

All this is not part of a deliberate scheme by unseen and powerful officials; it is a disconcerting by-product of the scale, complexity and interdependence of our society, its organisations and its technical resources. To match this, democratic processes themselves have to become more sophisticated and delicate, if as many decisions as possible are to be the result of consensus and compromise between a whole range of conflicting opinions; and new techniques need to be grafted on to the traditional representative system. Here lies a serious dilemma: on the one hand, people in a highly educated democracy consider that they have a right to a direct say in decisions which affect them and expect a rapid and reasoned response to their needs and protests. There is a strong current of individual and group vitality in society—witness the lively and continuous debate about housing, employment and social security—to which our representative system has not so far succeeded in responding fully. On the other hand, major decisions become more and more complicated in this technological age, as their consequences become increasingly far-ranging, interwoven and difficult to predict. A whole variety of specialised expertise is therefore needed to marshal the argument s and alternatives for major decision and it is extremely difficult to present these so that they can be readily understood by the average person.

Moreover it is not merely that the rationale of decisions taken tends to become less and less intelligible or acceptable to the electors, employees or other individuals whose lives may be drastically changed thereby. The decision-making bodies themselves, whether local or national, political or industrial, constantly grow larger, so that the focus of power within them becomes more remote and seems less and less sensitive and responsive to the needs of individual people. To the person 'on the receiving end', those who advise on, take or carry out decisions often appear 'faceless', arbitrary or irresponsible. Yet they are in fact individuals grappling with intricate responsibilities and choices, trying to do their job well—and frequently, in other contexts, 'on the receiving end' themselves.

Decisions have to be made, if society is not to drift or to disintegrate in times of rapid change; but major issues cannot at present be decided collectively by all those whose lives might be affected. Nevertheless, community work can be one way of opening up opportunities for decision-makers to be recruited from a wider social background; it could also extend the machinery for giving all those likely to be affected a chance of having their say, in such a way that they can *see* that any views they have expressed have been given due weight in the scales. If a well-balanced decision is then reached, and the grounds for it explained, it would be reasonable to expect it to be substantially accepted and supported.

Elected members themselves may sometimes find it difficult to understand the issues sufficiently or to weigh the consequences of alternative courses of action. Their control over decision-making may then be eroded, with power falling increasingly into the hands of groups of expert officials whose view of community needs is inclined to be a limited one. It may indeed be tempting for the expert in one specialised field to get into the habit of treating the individual 'layman' with disdain, forgetting that he has his own expertise of living, his own feelings of status and a clear idea of how he is entitled to be treated as a citizen. Yet the expert's special skill is a valuable asset and an important element in good decision-making in a technological society—but only one element, one part of a picture, the whole of which has to be seen in its proper proportion before a decision is reached. Experts may often be best qualified to say what alternative courses of action are feasible and what the consequences of each are likely to be; but at the next stage those whose lives will be affected by what is decided have the strongest claim to influence the decision itself, and may well resent the consequences of what elected representatives decide, unless they have been specifically consulted. This implies the need to encourage more receptive and more 'community-oriented' attitudes of mind on the one hand and constantly to improve the machinery for consultation on the other.

These processes are likely to be assisted if an elected council is ready to listen to any and every community group whenever its members' interests are at stake, however partisan or extreme its viewpoint may seem; it should also help for elected representatives, whether members of a local council or of a voluntary agency or community group, regularly to 'return to the grass roots' and so to remain sensitive to shifts in their constituents' points of view—no easy matter in times of rapid change and daily pressures. Community workers can make a contribution in partnership with elected representatives, rather than usurping their functions.

Response to community pressure

There has been some response to community pressure for a proper say in decisions—witness the issue of government Green Papers* for discussion of major proposals; the Skeffington report, *People and Planning*, and other committees of enquiry at national level; and a more receptive and 'open' attitude by those local authorities which are best attuned to the present climate, for instance in educational issues such as comprehensive schools or co-education, in housing and in closer relations with the mass media of communication. Other examples are the community councils suggested in proposals for local government reform in Scotland and Wales; references to consulting voluntary organisations and clients in a recent circular to local authorities asking for ten-year plans (1973–1983) for the development of their personal social services;† regular meetings of a London

* At least twenty have been issued by government departments since 1968, including four on economic and financial matters, three on tax questions, four on the health services and two on transport.

† Department of Health and Social Security Circular no. 35/72 of 31 August 1972. Paragraph 11 reads: 'It is very desirable that planning of the personal social services should take account of the views of voluntary organisations, which in many fields supplement and support the statutory services, and of the clients for whom the services are provided. The personal social services have a particularly intimate impact upon people's lives, and it is therefore important to allow for consumers' own views of needs to be expressed. Consultation with clients will be valuable, in particular, in providing evidence of the type, delivery and content of service needed, rather than the quantity. As the planning process develops in the future, the Secretary of State hopes that the views of clients and of voluntary organisations will increasingly be brought into consideration; and authorities are encouraged to give thought to methods of achieving this in the present planning exercise, and to take whatever steps in that direction they find practicable.'

borough council with representatives of all voluntary organisations in its area; joint management committees of tenants and councillors on some housing estates; the voice given in management to tenants' and residents' associations; and joint organisation of adventure playgrounds. But the change in these directions is not universal and the pace is often far too slow.

A suggested declaration of intent

A good many policy-makers, administrators and specialists working in the civil service, local government and elsewhere are well aware of the mounting pressure for direct consultation with the people who will be affected by particular policies under discussion. Many are increasingly sensitive to the consequences of failing to meet the need to take account of people's views through a genuine change from a paternalistic to a community-oriented attitude of mind. They know that it is no longer acceptable for them to work however devotedly *for* people; it is essential now to work *with* people. Those working in agencies of government and in large institutions need to be committed at all levels—and be seen to be committed— to the principle and practice of taking account of the views of people likely to be affected by a decision, before it is made. A declaration of intent on these lines would set the seal on existing practice or give the opportunity for a change of attitude where needed; and could at the same time introduce joint discussion on lines indicated below. It would then be natural for those who take the decisions to identify the people who would be affected by each decision and to take into account their views on the possible alternatives; bearing in mind also the ways in which those views were obtained and put in priority. At present every proposal put forward within a central or local government department or other official body is expected to state, as a matter of routine, the views of all other departments which might be concerned and the financial implications; and much time and energy is devoted to these 'internal' aspects. Community opinion is no less an essential component in the process of decision-making.

The need for joint discussions among councillors, officials and community group representatives

To give practical expression to this, elected members and officials of authorities at all levels should come together regularly for consultations, in order to discuss among themselves and with representatives of community groups such difficult issues as:

> the techniques for presenting clearly to 'laymen' concerned the alternative proposals on complex technical matters of planning and so on;

how people or groups likely to be affected by official proposals could most effectively come together to be briefed on the proposals and could crystallise or hammer out some consensus on the alternatives;

how such an agreed view of the best alternative could be presented so as to exert the maximum influence on decisions;

the processes through which elected representatives and officials could become more sensitive to community opinion in a rapidly changing social and technological scene;

how community groups in their turn could come to appreciate better the functions and difficulties of elected members and officials.

The principal aims would be both to encourage and develop a community oriented attitude of mind at every level of the bureaucracy and also to help community groups to understand the responsibilities of elected members and officials, particularly the difficulties of weighing and reconciling conflicting demands. A small working party would be required, after the issue of a declaration of intent, to decide how such consultations could best be planned. But existing training organisations such as the Local Government Training Board, the civil service training schemes and university departments of social administration, or related departments in a wide range of educational settings would be among the obvious vehicles for promoting community-based attitudes and extending skills. Nevertheless, some of us would argue that changes of attitude of this kind are likely to result only from changes in the balance of power.

Illustration: local planning

The Skeffington report of 1969 and the reactions to it illustrate the opportunities and difficulties of community participation in decision-making, in a field the complexity of which is in character with the way we live. The report proposed consultation at four stages of a development plan or of a local plan based on it: when it is announced that a plan is to be drafted; when surveys are made; third, when the choices for settling the problems of the area (e.g. a concentrated new town or expansion of selected villages or general development of the area) are published for comment and, fourth, when the solution favoured by the planning authority is set out in detail and before it finally decides. The report also suggested that community development officers be appointed to stimulate public interest and participation; that societies and groups in the area should be encouraged to set up a joint 'community forum' to exchange ideas on the planning issues and work towards a consensus of opinion; and that all available publicity techniques and skills be used to explain the proposals and problems to those living in or interested in the area.

To participate fully in this planning process, members of the local community need first to know about, then to study, understand and influence the strategic plan before it is settled, rather than waiting for more detailed local issues to arise which may well be prejudged by the main plan; and secondly to follow the projection of conditions in the area over the life of the buildings etc. in the plan, a leap of the imagination which professional planners are trained to take. However skilled the interpretation to the layman, there is no escape, in a complex field, from such demands, if the local community is to make its voice effectively heard.

Involving those affected in government decisions

The foregoing illustration is concerned with a local development plan in a circumscribed area, in which individuals, community groups, elected representatives and officials alike breathe similar air and focus their minds on the same problems. Clearly it is much more difficult for a local community to contribute effectively to the process of decision-making by the central government. Yet it is no less important to find means of bridging the distance between the central 'decision point' and those in each area of the country whose lives may be severely affected by national decisions.

It is sometimes supposed that government departments are reluctant to seek local views, consider these to be usually myopic, regard local consultation as a time-wasting obstacle to getting on with pressing tasks and tend to pay little heed to local opinion. It may sometimes appear to be simpler to take decisions 'in the ivory tower'; yet public pressure may well succeed in getting a decision re-opened, with the result that there is then much longer delay in getting something done than if community views had been sought in the first place. It would be timely to enlarge the field of consultation to include, for example, the location of industry; the social effects of road improvement as against similar costs incurred by restricting the use of motor vehicles in certain areas; or high-rise flats as against the lateral spread of cities and the longer journey to work; or devoting more resources to higher education as against increased provision for children under five.

Some suggestions for methods of consultation

The following methods and techniques for consultation, some already in use, are likely to be helpful. The list needs to be kept open and augmented in the light of experience.

More use of existing groups

The decision-makers could consult much more widely and systematically with the multiplicity of existing community groups and organisations, ranging from advisory and professional bodies, local councils and voluntary welfare or interest groups to groups speaking for consumers or mobilised for protest or community action. The purpose would be to thrash out local differences of opinion and reach some degree of consensus; and even if this fails, the process of listening to other views can sometimes make the final decision more acceptable to all interests concerned.

New local groups

When a proposal arises for decision and people affected are not active in local or functional groups which can mobilise opinion, a deliberate effort could be made to stimulate and focus community views on the proposal.

Neighbourhood councils

Local authorities might encourage more widely the setting up either of neighbourhood or ward councils or of functional groups devoted to working out a collective view on questions which affect their members. Both methods may help to ensure that a local authority takes the fullest account of community opinion in making decisions; and in both, community workers often have a valuable 'servicing' role, in stimulating and encouraging the groups to formulate their views on what ought to be done and in helping members of the local authority to see clearly the nature and the weight of community needs. Members and professional officers of local authorities themselves would naturally participate in local group discussions.

Local councils

Parish councils could be more fully used to test opinion, being the smallest of the traditional groupings, with a national association which could when necessary lobby the central or local authority. When district or county councils become more remote, in consequence of local government reform, members elected from wider areas, probably on party lines, will be known to very few of their constituents and the people of one locality may cease to feel that 'their member' can speak for them with close personal knowledge of their needs. Superior councils could sound opinion in the parish through its council, whenever their plans impinge on its life—and there is a strong case for insisting on this when housing, road and other plans are being prepared. The most acute social needs may well be found among people in cities; but the small town and the village community also need a voice.

Survey and publicity

When the central government or a local authority intends to take an initiative which will lead to change, it has a clear responsibility—if our system of government is to be seen to be genuinely democratic—itself to find ways of discovering directly the views of those who will be affected, through the techniques of social survey or otherwise,* and the department or authority should be prepared to declare its intention publicly, for discussion at the formative stage. Such methods would supplement, not exclude, consulting local organisations. Changes which cause even stronger local resentment, if imposed without first being explained and discussed, include the closing of schools, hospitals or public transport services and the diversion of roads or the siting of hostels for the handicapped.

The mass media

The mass media, press, television, radio and cinema could more strongly support the processes of consultation by giving more space or time to presenting central and local government proposals imaginatively, so as to bring out clearly the arguments for and against and to help those affected to make up their minds where the balance of advantage lies; and it is reasonable thus to aim at enlisting the resources and expertise of the media more directly in the interests of the community. In close concert with expert officials and elected members it should be feasible for the media to put any proposal vividly and objectively before those likely to be affected and to stimulate interest and discussion, leading naturally from the effects on individuals or groups to more general aspects. The local press has a key role to play in ventilating local issues which are coming up for decision; and local radio stations might well be vehicles for the expression of community interest and concern, provided that they represent all viewpoints. Other technical developments in communication are likely to extend the means available to a wide range of groups in the community to express their views; and could provide a debating area for extreme differences as well as moderate views.

Consultative documents

Decision-makers could more often issue consultative documents such as the government Green Papers, to put forward proposals on

* The suggestion made here is not met by the existence of public tribunals of enquiry which function only if published plans are opposed.

many issues of policy on which the relevant community is not always consulted at present but is vitally affected, such as the reform of the tax system, of social security benefits, of housing policy, of the health service, of the penal system and so on. Green Papers can be most valuable bases for better organised and informed community discussion—valuable not least to members of parliament or of local authorities in seeking to gauge accurately their constituents' views. Public corporations and nationalised industry—the BBC, telecommunications, the electricity and gas supply industries, etc.—could also in particular make use of this device, since their services are of close daily concern to virtually every member of the community. As a topical example, if the Post Office, the Electricity Boards or British Railways regularly explained in simple terms direct to users any move to increase rates and charges and also set out the alternatives (reduced services, higher taxes, etc.) and then considered any suggestions from users, through the existing users' or consumers' council, *before* deciding, some at least of the heat and indignation generated by such changes could be avoided.

Advisory committees

Advisory and consultative committees could be encouraged to select at least some of their own members and publicly to invite suitable people or organisations to come forward for selection or to suggest members. The open recruitment for manning the Scottish children's panels is an interesting example. This would be seen to give the community a voice in their composition.

Consultation as a routine

A regular routine for consulting those affected by decisions should be written into all planning and other legislation, regulations and powers which impinge on the quality of life. Three riders should be added.

Short- and long-term proposals Community groups should be consulted not merely on detailed development proposals of direct and immediate concern to every individual or to particular local or functional groups, but also on long-term policies which tend partially to predetermine more detailed decisions—and require a greater effort of application and imagination; this process should include the centralised services, prisons, hospitals, trunk roads, etc. where there is little *prior* consultation at present.

Timetable and time-limit As the pace of change accelerates, delays can bring confusion, even disaster. Strict and drastic, but not unreasonable, time limits need always to be set for all processes of consultation, within which interested community groups would have to organise themselves to respond effectively. But unacceptable delay, as a ground for failing to consult at all, should be viewed with scepticism.

Complexity and clarity Similarly, professional experts cannot plead that an issue of community concern is too complicated or too technical to be explained to laymen; they must always be required to set out their arguments briefly in plain language, if necessary with the help of those trained in communication skills.

Scale, efficiency and the community

Good reasons can no doubt be given for the increasing size of social institutions: a large school can afford to have a wider and more sophisticated range of teaching resources and aids; greater choice and opportunity for learning and for coping with learning difficulties. The same principle would apply to a large hospital. But if parents or patients are not to feel intimidated by or alienated from such large units then they need to feel that they are involved in the policy and operation of the school or hospital. This is even more important for the institutions of local government in view of the wide influence of their decisions upon the life of the community; the larger or more remote a local authority, the more pressing the duty of its members and officials to find means for genuine participation by its electors. For the central government, the duty is even more pressing and even less easy to discharge; the same duty rests upon the directors and managers of large industrial and commercial organisations and the officers of trade unions, indeed upon the leaders of any institution which decides questions of community concern. Managerial efficiency, economy in operation and comprehensive service are not the *most* important yardsticks with which to measure a social service or a political institution. These organisations may tend to operate increasingly in a vacuum unless they are seen to meet the needs of the community and to treat clients or electors as individuals in that process. If present organisations fail in this respect and if increasing size is not matched by more effective measures for community participation, then the whole question of scale may well require to be re-thought.

Conclusion

The scope of community work is wide, varied and in an early stage of development. Practice so far suggests that this variety will continue. But we think that there is a place for the trained community worker, particularly in situations where effective indigenous leadership has not yet emerged. Our general conclusion is that the community worker and community work itself will continue to be ineffective unless the basic tenets of community work attitudes are accepted by society in general and in particular by those responsible for planning administrative and organisational systems.

4 Community action

Introduction

One sector of community work to which no specific reference was made in the study group report, *Community Work and Social Change*, is community action. The emergence of the *ad hoc* groups characteristic of community action is a significant development which deserves detailed study, so as to consider both the ways in which community action initiatives arise and the problems and dilemmas faced by the groups. Certain features of the groups have led to an image being created which makes it difficult to be objective: 'their lack of professionalism, their operation outside formal structures and their readiness to take a frankly political stance have been hailed with scornful abuse by some (including some community workers) and with an almost messianic enthusiasm by others' (Holman, 1972a, p. 3).

The sub-group of the Community Work Group which compiled this chapter* did not attempt a full survey of the field. We have talked either as individuals or on occasions in group meetings to some of those who have been prominent in community action. We have collected a good deal of relevant material but have not been in a position to analyse it in detail or to take up with those who were involved points which arose in reading it. Many accounts are still versions of one side of reality or written on the surface of events with inadequate tools of analysis. In other respects the balance of the material has been fortuitous and it was not possible to obtain access to all that we wanted to study. Moreover, there has been no consensus within our own sub-group—perhaps appropriately for one concerned with community action—on whether it is desirable for such *ad hoc* groups to develop, or possible for them to be given support and resources not at present available to them; nor did we agree on their significance or what is likely to happen to them in the future.

Aims

Our specific aims in this chapter are four:

* The words 'we', 'our', 'us', etc. in this chapter generally refer to the sub-group. See also 'Method of working', pp. 2–3.

First of all, to obtain a working definition of community action, its characteristics and its relationship to other forms of community work. The term is used so widely that we must make our own use of it as specific as possible. This has to be undertaken against a background of related historical experience, to indicate how far community action expresses and embodies traditions in British society. We need also to examine those features of our society and those processes of change which make it more likely that community action will develop in the present situation.

Second, to discuss some of the most significant varieties of community action to be found at the present time, with an attempt to distinguish between them and point to goals, methods and tactics which are used by the groups and the resources which are available to them.

Third, to analyse community action at a number of different levels, taking into account the present view of community action groups held by local authorities, and other bodies, both statutory and voluntary, the people involved in the groups, the types of support they can expect, their achievements and some views about how success is achieved or failure is brought about.

Fourth, whilst no general summary of the earlier part is attempted, to consider issues which have a bearing on community action and the ways in which groups can be supported and helped to be more effective. This leads on to some conclusions.

Definitions

The term 'community action' has different connotations in the United States from those to be found in general in Britain. There it has commonly been used to refer on the one hand to action in the community, of whatever kind, action informed by a wide range of assumptions, undertaken by all manner of groups, with a wide range of objectives; and on the other, since the beginning of the War on Poverty, to action which had dissatisfaction and protest at its core. The term 'social action' is used more frequently to cover the latter.

An example of the first view is to be found in an article by Roland Warren (1964) in which he discusses formal groups in the community concerned with problems of health. The use of the term in this general way is also to be found in a recent study of the voluntary and statutory structure of community relations in Britain (Hill and Issacharoff, 1971; see also Armstrong, 1972). In his contribution to a Fabian tract, John Banks takes a similarly broad-ranging view of the groups involved. He says (Lapping, 1970, p. 4):

Community action seems to cover four main kinds of activity.
1. It can describe action by a minority pressure group pursuing redress or reform on behalf of others: examples are the Child

Poverty Action Group, Abortion Law Reform Association,
Release, and so on. 2. It can describe action by a minority
pressure group pursuing reform, particularly in the health and
welfare services, on behalf of themselves and others; examples
range from the Spastics Society, the National Association for
Handicapped Children or the Council for the Advancement of State
Education, to consumer societies. 3. It can describe the work of
minority groups primarily concerned with reform or changes on
behalf of themselves; the main examples here are the civic and
amenity societies. 4. It can describe the work of minority groups
whose main function is to provide a service to society not otherwise
provided, coupled with an interest in promoting reform to have
the service provided by an agency of government: some such
groups are mainly self help or mutual help; others, like the
young 'volunteer' agencies may have a social education role: yet
others may be primarily a form for expressing rejection of
society's values, or for achieving by direct action what society
has come to regard as impossible.

The aims he sees these groups pursuing are problem-oriented, that
is to say, 'they originate in response to a need in society', exerting
pressure on authority, and in consequence anxious to expand the
basis of their support.

The second view finds expression in a recent article by Richard
Bryant (1972, p. 206):

Community action may denote a particular approach to organising
local groups and welfare publics; an approach in which the
political impotence or powerlessness of these groups is defined
as a central problem and strategies are employed which seek to
mobilise them for the representation and promotion of their
collective interests.

Smith and Anderson (1972) take community action to be 'collective
action by people who live near each other who experience either
common or similar problems, which are usually those giving rise to
a common sense of deprivation.'

The first view covers such a wide field of activity as to include
almost any movement by any minority groups using any methods to
achieve change, and no doubt this use of the term will continue. Yet
the upsurge of protest in recent years, which has specifically claimed
the title 'community action', has features which allow it to be distinguished from other, more traditional reform movements. We therefore concentrate on the second and stricter definition and note that
it is put forward by works published in 1972 (the year in which we
write). The definitions quoted emphasise the collective nature of
community action, the poor (or deprived) taking action on their own

behalf, a location in a neighbourhood, and objectives framed in terms of overcoming political powerlessness.

Emergence

It would be a mistake to consider community action as a new phenomenon. It is in fact the re-emergence of a long historical tradition of people, brought together by the common recognition of a problem or a situation, striving to do something about it. However uncertain the hope, the eventual aim of many local organisations, political and industrial, has been to change the political and social structure of the country. At times such groups have attempted to increase their influence by promoting formal links such as federations, anticipating some recent developments in community action groups.

In the inter-war period, the activities of the unemployed, in what became a national movement, have some relevance for the present time. In general the issues had to do with poverty and living at a bare subsistence level, or below it, on statutory benefits or 'handouts'. Their aims were largely political and national in scope whereas this is less common among the community action initiatives at present. None the less they also operated within a local context in the form of putting pressure, which was usually resisted or discounted, on the structure of power and administration. Theirs was a political standpoint.

The change in social assumptions associated in Britain with the Second World War, the decline in the number of unemployed and the apparent lessening of poverty, combined with the lack of an effective voice for those who were still in poverty, meant that there was little continuous activity of this kind from 1939 until the late 1950s. There were exceptions: one of the most significant being the move by squatters into disused army camps and other places after the Second World War, when they were unable to find proper housing for themselves. Their problems were usually assumed to be short-term, and their action a response to issues (like housing) which would soon be resolved.

Clearly, community action is now much more widespread. The reasons for this arise from a growing awareness of certain characteristics of our present society. It is argued that as the complexity of life increases and the apparatus of administrative power becomes more pervasive, so there emerges a growing consciousness of a lack of individual power and a greater likelihood of injustices being perpetrated. Perhaps with a few exceptions, the social policies which are devised, often with specific needs in view, tend to disadvantage further those who are already at a disadvantage and assume that the present structure of power gives adequate access to the disadvantaged in deciding their own destinies and in having their grievances redressed. Many of the current discussions about 'participation' appear to regard it as some kind of panacea for these feelings and attitudes. In the partial view of those affected by their decisions, planners may appear to regard participation as a procedure which will either underwrite decisions that have already been made or, exceptionally, ask for opinions about policies under discussion. The point that needs to be made here is that these discussions are assumed to go on within the framework of decision-making determined by the planners, on their terms and with the information being provided in most cases by themselves.

The elements which can be distinguished in the present situation include: a consciousness of the remoteness of the structure of power, the growing complexity of the bureaucratic apparatus and the control which that apparatus has over people's lives and the main sources of information, and the growing dissatisfaction which these bring. As two American writers, Cloward and Piven (1969, p. 359), indicate:

> The growth of the bureaucracies of the Welfare State has meant the diminished influence of low-income people in public spheres. This has come about in two ways: first, the bureaucracies have intruded upon and altered processes of public decision so that low-income groups have fewer occasions for exercising influence and fewer effective means of doing so; and second, the bureaucracies have come to exert powerful and inhibiting controls on the low-income people who are their clients.

It might be thought that the British system of local government and parliamentary representation would counter the feelings of powerlessness and meet higher aspirations. However, in relation to the deprived, local government appears to possess three major shortcomings. First, there is little doubt that major local authority decisions which affect the everyday lives of people are taken with little consultation or conveyed to them at a very late stage. For instance, in a large Midlands city people whose homes might have been demolished to make way for a flyover did not receive notification until seeing a press report. Housing redevelopment and road-building schemes are liable to be agreed upon by officials and councillors without local residents (and such schemes are often directed at the deprived inner rings) really appreciating the full implications. Not surprisingly, this evokes bitter hostility towards local government.

Secondly, it is felt that local councillors often do not represent adequately the interests of poor sections of the community. Thus a recent research study commented on the 'inability of the politicians to provide reliable, continual and powerful advocacy of community interests and human needs during the process of [urban] renewal . . .' (Muchnick, 1970, p. 108). It is even claimed that councillors may sometimes serve to inhibit any radical solutions suggested by officials (Stuart, 1971). Despite this, it is not an uncommon experience for community workers to meet councillors who believe that they (and nobody else) are a sufficient vehicle for grievances (Wilson, 1970). No doubt there are many exceptions to the above generalisations yet, beyond question, the shortcomings of local government do act as a spur to community action.

Third, it should always be remembered that the British system of local government operates within the framework of an exceptionally centralised control of the total social capital expenditure; local authorities do not enjoy freedom to spend their own money on capital projects (nor, for that matter, on school milk), even if they are willing to do so.

These shortcomings raise questions about the much praised British 'democratic' local government system. Probably the democratic element has been over-emphasised, for the deprived appear to have few spokesmen in town halls. Nandy argues (1970) that councillors elected on a turnout of some thirty per cent do not represent the poor. 'They are responsible only to the most influential, the most articulate and most organised sections of the community'. Further, there are grounds for arguing that the two main political parties favour middle-class candidates by their selection procedures, with the result that, in a two-party system, the choice of alternative candidates, with whom one may or may not feel identified, does not exist for many people (see Hindess, 1971). Consequently, local government is not necessarily perceived as democratic or representative and help has to be sought through other means.

The rationale of our existing power structure is based on the concept of representative democracy under which citizens have access to those in charge of policy. By voting in elections it is assumed that the citizen can control what is provided for him and have access to the redress of his grievances. The reality suggests that citizens are often not in a position to know about or understand many regulations and rights which closely concern them. Further, it is virtually impossible to gain representation outside the two main political parties, so that for many citizens alternative policies do not really exist. In this context, therefore, it is necessary to challenge the validity of the assumptions which are made about local government and its effectiveness. The *status quo* stands on a particular interpretation of what that system provides. One of the ways of justifying community action, and implying that it will be more necessary in the future, is to point out how much more complex the experience of life has become.

There is a growing conflict, because of the time that can be given to these matters, between the two roles of the councillor as grievance-solver and as policy-maker. To regard the elected representatives in many cases as adequate channels of information is to ignore their concentration upon solving individual grievances. They are not in a position, given the way they are doing their jobs at the moment, to be able to make contact with more than a very small number of those whom they represent. They may not live in the area, and they may have only limited contact with it because of the demands made on the rest of their time, this in a situation where they are only part-time at the best.

The growing awareness by the poor of the extent of their relative deprivation; the apparent inability of social services and local government to provide radical solutions; and the powerlessness of many groups to remedy the ills which they band together to redress have combined to create a situation ripe for action. It is also important to remember the sense of injustice and deprivation that can be created by the activities of big businesses which are not subject to democratic control (see Tugendhat, 1971). Meanwhile a disillusionment with traditional party politics has caused those who wish to promote, or are adversely affected by, social change to seek alternative methods. In many cases they have turned to community action.

Features

Even a few years ago, in 1968, Robert Holman could write (pp. 645–7): 'Postwar social reform in Britain has frequently been strongly influenced by middle class pressure groups; rarely by pressure from the deprived themselves.' He went on to anticipate some of the developments that have taken place:

> In Britain so far, only 'respectable' clients have formed large-scale movements. There are extensive old age pensioners' organisations, but not one for the unemployed. But the birth of movements for the under-privileged is under way, and there is activity to mobilise the forces of unmarried mothers, the handicapped, immigrants and those in poverty. Moreover, the ground is fertile for their growth . . . Organisations of the poor appear to have two main advantages. First, their militancy, their threat, can be a more effective pressure on governments than the academic findings of middle class pressure groups. A comparison can be drawn with students and with the civil rights movement. Both represent the frustrated, the unheard, and both have found a hearing only when they resorted to militant tactics. It is true that the poverty marches in the United States have provoked some resentment, but there is no doubt that the demonstrations of the Welfare Rights movement have got results. Militant client movements in Britain would have little to lose.

Events have largely borne out the prediction. Sections of the under-privileged have organised themselves or participated in organisations directly identified with their situation. And as the quantity of community action has increased so has information about it which, in turn, leads to more initiatives elsewhere. Duplicated reports circulate between activists, several magazines or papers exist, and national conferences about community action are not unknown. Simultaneously sympathisers, such as the radical social workers who produce the magazine *Case-Con*, take an interest in and give support and publicity to community action. These sources of information, coupled with the experiences of members of the sub-group themselves, allow some features of community action to be identified.

Location

Although not confined to them, the growth of community action has been most apparent in what may be called socially deprived areas. Among their most important characteristics are housing conditions of overcrowding and a lack of amenities, a higher than average proportion of families receiving state supplements, a high incidence of large families and fatherless families, a lack of play space and recreational facilities, poorer health than in the population as a whole, relatively high numbers of delinquents and children received into public care, and probably inadequate social and public services. Individuals in severe poverty are also found in other locations but economic factors and, sometimes, social policy have forced the most deprived into concentrated and definable areas. Some of them have turned to community action as a means of protest against their enforced poverty.

The participants

Community action stresses the involvement of those who are regarded as poor or deprived. Their involvement, not just as members but as leaders and decision-makers, marks community action off from those organisations which see such people as clients. Indeed, some community groups would argue that traditional social work bodies and professional community workers who 'stimulate' a variety of groups are reinforcing deprivation by casting people into the position of recipient or client.

The involvement of the deprived, usually drawn from one neighbourhood or bound together by a particular circumstance such as being a claimant or an unsupported mother, is such that, given help and encouragement, they contribute significantly to and even control activities. Thus in reporting on Friends Neighbourhood House in Islington, Anne Power makes special mention (1972) of local mothers running playgroups and being on the committee of an adventure playground which negotiated with the Greater London Council.

Community action has also involved 'outsiders', persons not socially deprived themselves but who have discovered a close identification with and a commitment to persons in poverty. Sometimes they possess a strong political orientation and in some cases, for instance the squatting campaign in London, the role of political leaders has been crucial. These political connections are sometimes quoted as evidence that their activities are not genuine or legitimate. It must be countered that other community workers, social workers, councillors, and indeed local government officials and civil servants also hold political views which shape both the style of and the objectives of their actions. The difference is that community activists often make their political loyalties quite overt.

Students, too, may be politically motivated persons entering the community action scene. Criticisms of their effectiveness have been expressed (Holman, 1972b), but there is no question that student community action is widespread and is taking on an organisation and structure of its own.* Certainly, students and other activists may not experience the continual poverty of most residents in the areas where they operate. The involvement of students frequently provokes the question—what right have they to intervene? This question of legitimacy equally concerns every form of community action. Similarly, community groups are often asked how representative they are. The issues of legitimacy and representation are important; and there are no simple criteria for settling them. It is as wrong to assume that it is illegitimate for students to become involved as to accept without question the legitimacy of established pressure groups drawn from professional organisations.

Clearly the forms and sources of leadership in community action are at variance with accepted ideas of what leadership is and the kinds of people from whom leaders are usually drawn. The better educated and more financially resourceful are in a position to draw upon specific expertise, professional abilities and known contacts within 'the system' to block any threats to their interests. A pertinent example is the successful campaign which influential people waged against the proposed siting of the third London airport at Stansted. The unemployed, unmarried mothers, residents of twilight areas, do not possess the educational and social resources of such middle class leaders. Their strength rests in their understanding of what poverty means, the capacity to communicate with people in a like predicament and an anger stemming from the injustices and inequalities of society. But lacking the resources of traditional leaders they have to adopt tactics and approaches which may offend those used to achieving change by more established methods.

The economic and social weaknesses of the participants result in their emphasising another strength—the collective nature of their activities. They feel weak compared with the outside forces that operate against their interests, yet the localisation of community

* Student Community Action is a section of the National Union of Students with full-time officers and a magazine, *Scanus*.

action does promote a feeling of solidarity. As Anne Power (1972, pp. 4–5) aptly puts it:

> One tenant has no power with the landlord or council, but fifty have courage and have to be answered . . . They (local groups) have sprung up through people finding that not only do they know better than any expert what problems they face, but also that by getting together and organising they can tackle some of their problems and have an impact on the people who control their lives.

Objectives

Community action, then, involves the poor and others who identify with them, in developing an awareness of a common situation which is to be countered by collective action. Implicit in this development is a view of poverty and deprivation as inherent in the social and economic system and persisting because of the powerlessness of the deprived. A major objective, therefore, is to increase their power, to win some control over resources, some control over their own neighbourhoods and lives.

This may be a somewhat grandiose-sounding objective; it should not be misrepresented as implying that community action includes plotting a *coup d'état* to take over the established structures of local and central government. On the contrary, the victories sought are those immediately relevant to the deprived such as the opening of playgrounds, the provision of day care facilities, the improvement of housing. The objective is thus short-term as well as long-term, with short-term gains demonstrating that the poor can define their needs and take steps to use society's resources to meet them. Occasionally the gain is implemented by groups employing full-time workers to run activities, such as staff of adventure playgrounds and playgroups. However, the employment of the worker remains in the hands of the group, so both the establishment of the activity and its continuance are an expression of achievement by people often regarded as worthless or lacking in ability.

Strategies

As community action defines its problem as that of powerlessness, as it has little access to the links commonly established between government and traditional voluntary bodies, as it rejects the 'client' label and relationship employed by local authority departments, it is hardly surprising if the strategies and tactics adopted are somewhat different from normal practices and even provoke some resentment.

Richard Bryant (1972, p. 208) postulates two sets of strategies as characteristic of community action—bargaining and confrontation strategies:

Bargaining strategies are conventionally employed in situations where negotiation is possible between the various interests involved and the framework for action is defined by the institutionalised processes of formal and pressure group politics. The tactics adopted by community groups, operating in bargaining situations, may embrace the lobbying of councillors, MPs and prestigious public figures, petitions, and information and publicity campaigns directed at the mass media. In contrast, confrontation strategies are employed in situations where a polarization of interests exists and the conventional processes of political representation are viewed, by community groups, as being unproductive or dysfunctional for the pursuit of their ends.

Confrontation strategies may be accompanied by rent strikes, demonstrations, sit-ins and other overt expressions of conflict, but not inevitably so. It is as mistaken to regard community action as wholly dependent upon overt conflict tactics as it is to condemn its participants as 'arrogant, thrustful and aggressive conflictmongers'. (Hodge, 1970, p. 78). In fact, although community activists do recognise conflicts of interests between different sections of society, they are prepared to be advocates, agitators, advisers, publicists, publishers, protesters, service providers, indeed to take on any role which furthers the objectives of community action.

Some community groups sustain action over a long period. Many others, because they arise from sudden popular protest over a specific issue, are short-lived. The short term is sometimes considered an advantage. It is argued that such groups will not become institutionalised and lose their original drive and objectives. The tendency to respond rapidly but briefly to new situations can mean that a large number of people are involved at different times. As Jan O'Malley says about Notting Hill (Lapping, 1970, p. 31):

The struggles on housing, on road conditions, on inadequate play space, have led to limited victories and often to frustration and defeat, but over the months, networks of people have grown up, people who mostly have no interest in regular meetings but who will join together on an urgent issue or who will give time and energy to a regular activity for children.

On the other side, it is claimed that short-term bursts will inhibit the development of national, co-ordinated community action with an influence on national policy.

Community action and community development

The identification of the main features of community action allows it to be distinguished from community development. Peter Hodge

(1970, p. 69) has defined the latter as 'a *process* which aims to achieve through *consensus*. It is client-centred and based on the self-determined goals of the community groups with which the worker is involved. The worker has an enabling role and brings to bear on the problems requiring solutions certain resources.'

Obviously, community development is close to community action but its mode of operation (in contrast to community action) is the sending in of workers by an outside body which is distinct from local residents. In the case of the Coventry Community Development Project the outside body, set up by the local authority, consisted of the chairmen of the main local authority departments, two further councillors, and nominees of the central government and established voluntary organisations. Most important, it was this body which exercised the primary control over selecting the workers. Bennington, in an article on the Coventry project (1971), points out that its development 'will be in full consultation with local people' but consultation is very different from control. In community action the capacity to appoint, dismiss and define the role of workers lies within the group itself. The definition of needs and solutions in members' own terms rather than those of outside organisations is vital to community action whether or not a full-time worker is employed.

In practice the distinction between community development and action may be blurred. For instance, in a paper prepared for us by Julie Hiscox in 1972 it is shown that the Young Volunteer Force is a community development organisation which has high level discussions with co-operative local authorities before sending in a team. Yet the young workers who are drafted in may possess (or come to) an analysis of society very similar to that of community activists, may adopt similar objectives, and may decide that their role is to provide resources for local community action groups. Similarly, the Haringey Family Advice Centre (which broke away from the Family Service Units organisation in order to bridge the structural gaps between caseworkers and clients) operates through families and full-time workers making joint decisions about activities, and looks to a *future* position when 'workers would be employed by clients to contribute specialised knowledge towards ends delineated by families. We would have moved from client participation to client power' (1970).

The main features of community action have now been described in terms of its location, participants, objectives and strategies. No doubt, many other organisations adopt tactics similar to those mentioned (for instance, protesters against proposed airports have resorted to militancy). No doubt, other groups are situated in localities (such as local amenity groups). It is worth noting that the groups concerned may frequently be of mixed composition in regard to class, income and access to political decision-making. For example, a property development company may buy up a block of old-fashioned flats and force out the tenants who, even though they may be middle class, may also be poor and powerless in the context. Nevertheless we believe that an outstanding characteristic of community action is the involvement of the socially deprived—the very ones usually excluded from other organisations—in action to improve their situation.

Varieties

Notting Hill is the best known focus of community action in Britain yet, as Martin Adeney points out (1970): 'Notting Hill is only unique for the steady stream of publicity it manages to achieve'. Many other forms of community action exist outside Notting Hill and London. In the central areas of most large cities and in some council estates can be found a variety of action groups. These include tenants' associations, housing action or advice centres, playgroups, play space projects, community workshops, welfare rights campaigns, information shops, community newspapers and many others. Some are spurred into life against authority or power, against the local council, against property developers with large schemes which have no place for existing residents, against private landlords or large bureaucracies. Here the actions are taken to oppose those forces bearing on the community that, wittingly or not, perpetuate deprivation and powerlessness. Other groups join together to set up an alternative to the way things are done. This can be radical and threatening, as with the free school movement. It can irritate and harass, like many community news-sheets; it can also add to the established life of a neighbourhood by providing services or amenities like playgroups and information centres. Most community groups concentrate on their own cities but occasionally efforts are made to link groups, as in the Conference of Neighbourhood Agitators, the National Federation of Claimants' Unions and the City Poverty Committee.

Clearly, community action has many varieties and in this section we propose to illustrate some of them. Most groups are firmly located within a small neighbourhood but recipients of social security benefits and unsupported mothers are examples of people in a similar relationship to society but drawn from a wider geographical area who have combined to take action. Hence our first example will be claimants' unions. Welfare rights and housing needs have provided the focus for much action so the second and third examples will mention these. The involvement of outsiders, often with a political commitment, will be demonstrated in the work of squatters and student community action. Lastly, mention will be made of efforts to communicate within the community action world. Needless to say, the examples given do not constitute a comprehensive typology of community action but simply illustrate what does happen.

Claimants' unions

The aims of claimants' unions are explicitly stated and are wide ranging. The Birmingham Claimants' Union states that it is 'a democratic association of persons who have received supplementary benefit ... in the last five years and of all persons relying on means-tested benefits for their existence'. Its constituency is therefore unsupported mothers, the sick, the disabled, the unemployed, old people and low income families. The Birmingham branch was set up in 1968 by a small group of people, two of whom were social work students at Birmingham University who had previously known unemployment. They called meetings to consider grievances such as waiting times at social security offices, the need for a 'claimants' wage slip' and a winter heating allowance. Over a period of time the main action of the Union has been to fight claims on behalf of its members, and to press for changes in policy. Thus the constitutional aim of the Union is 'to fight for the interests of all claimants by collective action and to provide the services claimants need to obtain their rights'. The aim is directed towards an improvement in the situation of claimants, both financially and also from the point of view of individual status, simply because the whole apparatus of claiming and receiving benefits implies 'second class' citizenship. Claimants' unions work by a system of collective action, a traditional trade union approach, on behalf of the individual with a grievance against the system. Some have also taken initiatives with strikers although these have not been well received by the unions involved.

Claimants' unions have gained success at two levels. One is in fighting individual cases and the other is in discussing practical arrangements within the offices where people claim benefits. The movement has not yet made a significant impact on national policies about poverty and unemployment.

In contrast to many community action groups, those like claimants' unions can continue in existence for an indefinite period simply by providing services for their members and by obtaining some amelioration of unpleasant conditions. But it is doubtful whether they can retain their early dynamism without going beyond this to formulate some ideology which is capable of attracting sufficient support to achieve a significant impact. The only alternative course of action open to them would appear to be to encourage a deepening sense of deprivation, possibly to the point of inculcating hostility, from which much more militant strategies involving overt conflict with 'the system' might emerge.

The existence of alternative strategies can promote divisions. First of all those who have had their wrongs redressed, if membership is seen for what it can provide individually, may see less reason to remain within the organisation. Second, some of those who become leaders in the elections held early in the course of a union's existence may not be suited to the organisational demands and the changes in policy in which the union is involved. Third, claimants' unions have been involved with various left-wing student groups, some of whose members are eligible for membership of the union on the criteria set out in Birmingham and these may well be far more preoccupied with general issues of policy and fighting 'the system' than they are with individual grievances and needs.

In one example about which information was received the claimants' union split up. Those who were not students dropped the term 'union' from their title and operated entirely in the field of individual grievance-solving. The students who were excluded from this organisation then attempted to set up another union in the same town. Problems of manipulation and a great diversity of purposes are, therefore, likely to arise. In fact the group of claimants which dropped the term union is now operating, in its grievance procedures, by making distinctions between what it takes to be deserving and undeserving cases. So the group acts on principles of less eligibility hallowed by the nineteenth century reformers of the poor law.

Facts such as these often depress and surprise those with a strong ideological commitment to community action. Along with the ideology and commitment may come much naive thinking and the people who in one situation are the oppressed may, in another, become the oppressors. There is a vivid illustration of this in Alinsky's *The Professional Radical* (1970, p.53): 'Some of the fruit ranchers in California steam around in Cadillacs and treat the Mexican American fieldhands like vermin. Know who those bastards are? They're the characters who rode west in Steinbeck's trucks in *The Grapes of Wrath*.' The social attitudes of the deprived may be as primitive and judgmental as are those of other groups in society.

The National Federation of Claimants' Unions, based in Birmingham, has had its ups and downs and at least one leader of claimants has campaigned nationally outside the existing federated structure, having clashed with other leaders over the priorities of the campaign. As against the extremely local flavour of much community action, which is often criticised for being *too* local, the claimants' union provides a considerable contrast.

Welfare rights

Claimants' unions have not been alone in furthering the rights of claimants. Welfare rights stalls and shops, run by various organisations, have multiplied in recent years. They bear some similarities to claimants' unions: they publicise rights to benefits, ensure that applicants are treated fairly by officials, work for the abolition of secrecy (as with the secret A and other codes used by social security offices), and call for higher benefits. However, they do not restrict member-ship to claimants and do not possess such an explicitly political framework.

Welfare rights campaigns do appear to have spread information and to have ensured that some of those eligible for benefits actually obtained them. But their limitations have been recognised (Bradshaw, 1970):

> Even if we achieve welfare rights without a massive backlash it should not be exaggerated as a solution to poverty. As I have said, it does nothing about power and alienation and as far as money goes the achievement of full entitlement to local authority means-tested benefits is a pathetic end. What it might achieve, however, is a realisation on the part of the social services of an ideal of service rather than one of exclusion. For instance, jog the Children's Department into being more daring and imaginative with its preventive resources under Section I of the Children and Young Persons Act 1963, let Housing know that tenant participation is not dangerous anarchy but a possible positive help, that the Ministry of Social Security should no longer be unpleasantly protective of its resources but generous, even kind and thoughtful. All in all it is a move away from a self-referral system to a positive approach to go out and find needs, to create a situation where the relationship between clients and officials is entered into out of mutual respect with rights and responsibilities which can be enforced on both sides.

Housing action

In the sphere of council housing there is a long history of tenants' associations. Not all such associations can be regarded as undertaking community action and Goetschius (1969) describes those whose main concerns were with recreational, social welfare and social facilities. However, there is a history of resistance to rent increases while, more recently, other associations have challenged redevelopment plans; examples are the Housing Action Group in Moss Side, Manchester, and the St Anne's Tenants' and Residents' Association in Notting-ham. Council tenants usually have the advantage of being grouped together in fairly large numbers and have a public landlord who can be easily identified. Both these factors, which make the organising of a group more feasible, may be denied the tenants of private landlords. However, some evidence does suggest that successful community action can be undertaken by private tenants.

Tenants' associations have worked to improve their housing condi-tions, to obtain re-housing, to influence redevelopment plans, to prevent evictions and to stop rent increases. Other, even more dis-advantaged, people have similarly striven for their 'housing rights'.

The organisation formed by the homeless families placed in Chaucer House, Southwark, resorted to withholding rent, demonstrations and denying officials access to the building in an attempt to persuade the Council to close the unit and to re-house them in more tolerable conditions.

The Chaucer House tenants, knowingly or not, were using some of the tactics employed previously by homeless families at the King Hill Hostel of Kent County Council. Here, as in many such hostels, wives and children were given a roof but husbands were sent off to fend for themselves. The times at which they could visit their families were severely restricted. The persistent protests of the families, aided by sympathetic public reaction, eventually resulted in a change of policy. Like other tenants' associations, the King Hill group demonstrated that the weak, if organised, could bring influence to bear on powerful institutions.

The squatters

Reference has already been made to the squatters' campaign, notably in East London, the history of which may be open to various interpretations. This was an example of a group which was formed to engage in activities that would draw public attention in a dramatic way to the plight of homeless or slum families. To quote from the report of K. G. M. Smith, prepared for this sub-group in 1972:

Attention was to be focused on the observed inadequacies of the official bodies, responsible for assisting such families in making use of resources available to them; more precisely, the existence of thousands of unoccupied houses under the control of local authorities which the squatters felt could easily be utilised to satisfy this housing need. Besides highlighting these believed deficiencies in the way local authorities executed their duties, the campaign was intended to act as a catalyst which would bring about widespread and spontaneous squatting, hopefully on a scale witnessed after the Second World War. Such squatting would be supported and encouraged by bodies similar to the East London squatters.

Redbridge was selected as the stage where the confrontation with authority would be acted out, after careful inspection of its development plans had revealed that the multi-million pound redevelopment scheme in the Borough would mean the compulsory acquisition and eventual demolition of approximately 1,000 houses, many of which had, at that time, been standing empty for over a year, and some would be unoccupied for up to five years. These facts were used to good effect by the squatters as part of their policy of publicly discrediting the actions of the Redbridge Borough Council. Another reason why Redbridge was chosen was because of the unpopularity of the redevelopment scheme amongst local residents and organised bodies.

It might be mentioned at this stage that no approach had been made to the Redbridge Council by the East London squatters before the campaign had begun, to sound out the attitude of the Council concerning the use of empty and potentially empty properties. But from other preliminary soundings with different authorities the feeling was that this would be of no value. Of course, it must be remembered that the whole campaign was aimed at the problem throughout the whole of London, so there had to be a welter of widespread publicity to enable such a climate of opinion to be created as would encourage widespread squatting.

The question of which families to use for occupying the empty houses caused an early divergence in views amongst the squatters. The majority view (which was to prevail) was that any family in need which came forward willing to squat should be accepted. The other view advocated careful selection of families that would be capable of withstanding the mental and, indeed, physical stress which was expected to be generated by opposition to their squatting, throughout possibly months ahead.

The general plan of the campaign was to be executed in three stages: Stage 1 would be a brief occupation of property somewhere in East London to publicise the opening of the campaign; Stage 2 would be an occupation of longer duration (24 hours) to test official reaction and the operative mechanics of occupation; Stage 3 would be the actual prolonged operation involving the installation of squatting families in unoccupied properties within a chosen London Borough.

The roles of two of the main participants in the squatting campaign illustrate the importance of leadership from outside in community action initiatives. They had already had clashes with officialdom and learnt from these, and used tactics of direct confrontation to attempt to bring about change.

The whole of this case study illustrates one of the strengths that community action groups have in their relations with official bodies. This is the vulnerability of such bodies to information being circulated about them which shows them up in a bad light. In place of the monolithic structure which some radicals see when they look at established institutions, this showed how, by using techniques of arousing and focusing public opinion and with a strong case about the under-use of housing, a group can bring about significant changes of policy. This is, in effect, what the squatters did. All kinds of tactics could be used to question the credibility and the sincerity of local councils and a particularly striking case of this arose when it was discovered during a campaign that although the council had been compulsorily acquiring property to demolish it and redevelop the area they did not have planning permission for this redevelopment scheme. A newspaper article about the campaign said that it would be 1976, i.e. over six years, before some of the houses were likely to be demolished. Ironically the redevelopment scheme was stopped in its tracks in 1971 when the Minister responsible rejected the whole development plan. The techniques used by the squatters included discussion and bargaining with representatives of the Council; there was one occasion when councillors, police and squatters brawled when the squatters attempted to raise the issue. A difference of view within the Council was apparent here since some moderates did not desire a confrontation and some interpreted such incidents as plainly damaging to the squatters' generally peaceful public image. The differences in the attitudes among the leadership developed not so much at the outset but in response to the situations that arose.

The squatters can look back with some satisfaction on the results of their campaign in Redbridge. More use is being made of vacant council property, there has been an increase in the return from rents previously lost through the houses being empty, and procedures generally have been improved. This is perhaps a good example of providing the authorities with a motive, i.e. greater economic efficiency, which accords with the needs of people in that area. Contrary to the hopes expressed at the time, however, homeless families have not taken to squatting in significant numbers. At the same time it could be argued that this is now less necessary. The effect of militant struggle in one area may lead to the feeling that 'it can happen here' in other areas, and thus make the adoption of better practices much more likely. More councils have made agreements with squatters' associations, and this has helped to house more families. For example, in Tower Hamlets the agreement makes available to the association empty properties scheduled for redevelopment which have lives of at least twelve months before demolition, and these are used for housing families from within the Borough. In fact the association carries out repairs and attempts to recoup the cost by charging the occupying families a reasonable rent. In a number of ways therefore, organisations which set out with extremely radical intentions can end, as in this case, not necessarily by losing their radicalism but by acting in ways more suited to housing associations. There is nothing amiss in this progression.

Student action

Student groups provide other examples of outside people going in ostensibly to support local groups. An example of student involvement from Birmingham illustrates some of the problems (Barr, 1971): An early decision was to mount a Festival, in part to raise the morale and restore the dignity of a community depressed by its environment. In practice a programme of events for the adults including street parties, concerts, dances, debates, was organised whilst for the children a play scheme was operated for the three week period of the event. Whilst for its duration it appeared that the levels of involvement were reasonably high, particularly for events organised at a street rather than district level, results of attempts to establish a committee of locals to organise a similar event for the coming summer were a demonstration of the lack of a lasting impact. Indeed, closer examination revealed a feeling of bitterness on the part of many locals that so many resources had been expended on activities which they felt to be irrelevant to their needs.

A student involvement in a rent strike offers a second example.

Though the strike was initiated by a group of local residents without any interference from outsiders, as it progressed the need for support from persons with access to informational and financial resources was clear. Without such assistance it is unlikely that the strike would have achieved significant proportions. It is equally true, however, that these same people introduced into the situation a manipulative element . . . Inadvertently the support group adopted too much responsibility for the progress of the strike and in doing so removed the initiative from the strikers. Rather than the action providing an educative experience of self-help, it created a situation where local people were dependent on the skills and abilities of the supporting group. The strike lasted for about six months with around seventy different families actively participating at different times. Relative to the length of the action and the risks taken by the tenants the outcome was bitterly disappointing. A promise was drawn from the council that half of the area would be demolished two years ahead of schedule. This was called a victory. In fact the experience of the strike was for the tenants one of disillusionment. It had not produced the 'decent homes at fair rents' which had been the basic demand of the strikers nor had it significantly improved standards of maintenance of the properties in which they were still living. When no firm date had ever been given for the final demolition of the area, a promise that it would be brought forward by two years was not very meaningful. Strikers had been drawn from all over the area; the fact that half of them were to gain nothing was bitterly demoralising. Yet another agency—the politically motivated students—had failed to provide effective assistance in improving conditions and in the eyes of many local people was guilty of pursuing its own political ends to the exclusion of the real interests of the community.

The initiatives were thought by the groups promoting them to be assisting the community to meet its needs; yet they helped in fact to add to the demoralisation of a community which was already under great pressure because of its environment.

It is thus not just intentions but, rather, perceptions of priorities that are tested. The students were offered a house as a base which they felt they had to use, but its running took a lot of time and resources. This raises an important question: if resources are offered, whether for community action or community work, do we ask if they are relevant to the needs that have to be tackled or do we take the easy way out and accept them hoping that they will be useful? These are questions of concern to more than community action groups.

Communication

All kinds of groups and organisations are being set up to provide information about new developments and new organisations. One recent example is the group of planners who have started a magazine called *Community Action*, the first issue of which came out in February 1972. They state in this that their basic concern is 'that the lives of low-income groups are being planned actively or by default without their agreement or participation. Central government shows no commitment to tackling the basic issues of social injustice or inequality and local government policies can often be to the further detriment of low income groups.' Their objective is to circulate a magazine which will provide information about what is going on throughout the country so that the groups they support 'can oppose ill-conceived policies, propose alternative solutions and obtain a greater role in formulating and implementing policies which affect the lives of their members'. They go on to say, in a way that reflects a point already made, that 'community action alone may not result in major shifts in the distribution of resources but it can lead to increased political action which is necessary to achieve significant changes in society'.

Here the term is used to describe an activity by outsiders wishing to be involved rather than any 'grass roots' recognition of the need for such a magazine.

The immediate and specific achievements of some groups lead to the conclusion that community action has a continuing relevance in Britain. One view is that community action can only achieve local and immediate gains whereas another, at the other end of the spectrum, is that by making politically aware those who have previously been inactive, changes in the structure of British society could be brought about. However, both sides would agree that community action will not lead to Utopia via an overnight revolution.

In our conclusion we make no attempt to sum up the material that has been examined earlier. We are concerned here to look at questions and issues of special relevance which have a bearing on the existing place of community action and what is required (assuming this is desirable and possible) to give it a greater relevance and effectiveness in the future. We therefore pose questions about community action and the ways in which the range of activities under this head are likely to develop in the future. The first point is to consider how successful community action has been as a means of bringing about social change. How far is it able to meet the demands of those who organise in community action groups?

Success

Community action has promised more than it has performed but it has made itself a role outside the official structure of co-ordination, consultation and social planning. Some examples of specific achievements can be listed:

1.   The Housing Action Centre in Islington persuaded the local authority to change its policy in order to accept responsibility for re-housing tenants in furnished accommodation from a redevelopment area. Anne Power adds (1972, p. 7): 'This change is more than a major victory for the tenants; it is the beginning of answerability to the people directly affected for policies drawn up without consultation. It also marks a new departure in Islington housing policy—a better chance of a flat for those most in need, be they furnished tenants, black citizens, large families, or evicted.'

2.   There are a number of examples of groups causing changes in planning decisions. Residents' Associations in the Rhondda protested so strongly that the Council withdrew its original plans.

3.   Collective action has served to give a voice to those who were not heard as individuals. The claimants' unions have not only won *de facto* recognition as the representatives of members, but are increasingly turned to for statements by the mass media.

4.   The claimants' unions maintain that they have both enabled members to receive their rights and caused officials to treat claimants in a more dignified manner, to humanise the conditions of offices, and to improve the ways in which services are provided.

5.   Some groups claim that involvement enables participants to re-define their own situation in ways that avoid the personal or moral condemnation of the poor. In Haringey, a group challenged the 'problem family' concept which appeared to determine the way in which social workers treated local families. Once the families were drawn into a community project they were able to regard their situation not primarily as the result of personal inadequacy but of environmental deficiencies which they could help to counter by acting together.

6. Perhaps the most important, albeit intangible, achievement is that of politicising powerless people. Some workers see *their* role as political; others see it as making other people political (while others do not see their work in political terms at all).

Many of the failures of community action groups seem related to a lack of resources in terms of money, influence and expertise. Yet some succeed in the midst of many disadvantages. Gerald Popplestone in a study of successful action by private tenants (1972) makes some points which may have a more general application:

> Firstly, the tenants were in an unequal relationship with their landlord. Secondly, the injustice of the situation and the possibility of alleviation by collective action was made clear to them by activists. Thirdly, the concentration of tenants in one small location and the sharing of similar grievances facilitated joint action. Fourthly, specific and obtainable goals were set—the lowering of rents and repairs to the property. Fifthly, the selection of tactics—via legal machinery and demonstrations—which gained early victories and embarrassed the landlord. Sixthly, the availability of outside resources in the form of a solicitor, sympathetic pressmen, and a political group.

Anne Power, in her account of community action (1970, p. 6), offers six specific conditions that may conduce to success: a very direct problem that appealed to everyone in the area; resultant strong feeling and a desire to participate; inexperienced, inept council; antagonistic housing department; an inflammatory issue that the council did not want publicised; and a very locally based organisation.

Whatever the particular reasons for success, it is true to add that the line between success and failure is a thin one. The continued existence and strength of community action can arise from frustration when the desired rights are not given, but it can also fail through lack of credibility, if it continues to be unable to achieve its ends. It has been suggested that failure may be not just an inevitable but a desirable experience, providing greater knowledge and, properly used, more determination to succeed.

There is one further reservation that we must enter: not all community action is always incontestably 'right'. Examples might include 'blacks go home' activities or a local campaign to prevent a house in a particular street from becoming a hostel for mentally sub-normal people or ex-prisoners or drug addicts. However, even in these cases one must beware of viewing the action of local groups too exclusively from outside or with the too facile assumptions of liberal middle class attitudes. It is easy to condemn a working class organisation when it aims to prevent a house in its area from becoming a hostel for ex-prisoners; but its members may quite legitimately be drawing attention to the already high concentration of social problems within their area and pressing that more favoured areas should bear their share.

Implications of success

Successes can pose problems for community action. The squatters successfully caused some local authorities to use unoccupied houses while, in addition, some squatters were prepared to act as agents for one council, taking over and administering property. It could be argued that it was not the squatters' role to do the job of the council, that as council agents they would change their relationship with the homeless, and that they would have less time and inclination to pursue their original tactics in other local authorities. Certainly a split appeared in the squatters' ranks. Similarly, when considering welfare rights and the provision of information it may be that once the need has been demonstrated it is in the interests of the local authority to ask the group to continue to circulate information and to subsidise it. In this way a kind of natural history of organisations could be charted, relevant alike to both radical and orthodox groups. The charismatic leaders who start the thing off may be succeeded by the organisers and administrators who carry it on. The lions are succeeded by the foxes, and a subtle change of emphasis takes place once a stake in society has been achieved. For instance, the organisation in Woodlawn, Chicago, was essentially a people's organisation when it started, deliberately avoiding any links with existing official bodies such as trade unions, but later it could be argued that it became part of the power structure, bargaining along with organisations of very different kinds for a share of the resources which the metropolitan administration could provide (see Alinsky, 1970).

It would seem that the dilemma facing groups with some expectations of obtaining resources is precisely of this kind. If the money is accepted then what one informant called 'the bribery of respectability' gets to work. What began as a protest on matters of principle or ideology or arising from unbearable conditions, can become another form of service provision. On the other hand, it can be argued that involvement in service provision is a way in which previously powerless people begin to exercise some influence and control over the shaping of their own lives and neighbourhoods.

As organisation gets better the leadership of certain people is bound to assume a greater significance than where it is completely flexible. Clashes of personality may arise in the early stage and where this happens the 'processes of democracy' may be tantamount to going through the form without paying attention to its substance. Democracy can be seen as 'equality of commitment', and the bar to participation may be a high one, investing the power of making decisions in a small number only who are very active. There may be variations on this theme which give more power to the constituency and others which concentrate power effectively in the hands of some of the activists.

Local authorities The rise of community action is often the consequence of protest against the actions (or lack of them) of local authorities. Hence some comments are necessary on the relationship between the two.

Generally speaking local authorities do not give community action groups the respect that their serious intentions merit. They tend to be disregarded, treated with extreme caution or fobbed off because of the fear that if they are given any kind of recognition they will take advantage of this to disrupt the existing system. Some participants in community action report that officials obviously wish they did not exist despite the fact that they reach and serve deprived people more fully than the local authorities. These regard interaction with such groups as an activity outside their normal work and clearly wish they could be left to get on with their job in the time-honoured way. A poll of councillors in Kensington, as reported by Geoffrey Moorhouse (1970), said they favoured organisations like WRVS and other orthodox and conventional groups and not tenants' associations or the Notting Hill Community Workshop. The sub-group believes this attitude to be widespread amongst local authorities.

It is possible to identify some of the tactics used by local authorities* against community action. The first is to refuse to recognise their right to negotiate with or even approach the local authority, by asserting that the groups are not accountable to a constituency or represent but few people. Accountability is an issue to which community activists must give more attention but it is noticeable that local authorities rarely use it as a reason for not dealing with more respectable organisations. In one case, a tenants' association very quickly enlisted several hundred members and was able to persuade the housing committee of the local authority to include representatives of the association in a joint committee to consider the inadequacies of housing policy. As the representatives devoted themselves to gathering evidence for the committee they had to neglect their previous emphasis on building up membership. When membership did decline the housing committee brought into question the status of the representatives and the joint committee was discontinued. Support from the local authority might have enabled the tenants' association to maintain numbers and document cases; instead the opportunity was taken to side-step the combined investigation of poor living conditions.

* i.e. both elected members and officials, especially when interacting on one another.

Second, those versed in community action will be familiar with the tactic of delay. Whether asking for information or financial resources, letters can take weeks or even months to be answered. The eventual replies ask for extra details about the group's own finances and activities. The application for funds just misses the committee and has to wait several weeks for the next. The subsequent committee has a very long agenda and the application or whatever the group wishes to be raised has to be left, referred back for further information, or passed to another committee. No doubt local authorities are very busy but long delays will not make social deprivation decrease, even if it is hoped that the wait will make the community groups go away.

Third, planning permission (or its refusal) is a powerful weapon which local authorities can employ to encourage or discourage the development of voluntary organisations. Community action frequently focuses on an adventure playground or the use of property (as for a housing action centre) and the refusal of planning permission can be a severe blow. Of course, appeals can be made against decisions but the groups may be hard pressed to find the expertise and resources necessary to pursue them.

Fourth, local authorities can discriminate against community action groups by refusing their applications for financial grants. If the groups decide that they want to run playgrounds, day care centres, employ full-time workers, etc., they have to seek the resources from outside their own limited means. A common complaint is the unwillingness of local authorities to help while, more recently, some groups have argued that local authorities have not informed them about, or backed their applications for support under, the urban programme. The rejected applicants can express great bitterness at the denial of funds to the deprived when local authorities spend so much more on projects which aid the more wealthy and powerful sections of society. Local authorities receive many applications from voluntary societies but we believe that much greater priority should be given to organisations which involve the deprived.

The identification of these tactics does over-cast local authorities in the role of 'the baddies' against 'the goodies'. Of course, some authorities do recognise the value of community action and in others there are individual councillors and officials who lend their support. None the less, the common experience is to find them hostile or indifferent to actions outside the normal local government way of doing things. The consequences are serious. Rebuffed by authority, community action may resort to the militant tactics which are so much resented. Worse, the mechanisms which perpetuate deprivation are reinforced. The poor are denied access to the means of improving their own conditions. Councillors and officials miss the opportunity to appreciate more fully the needs of deprived areas. A premium is placed upon policies which have little relevance to many people and which underwrite the inappropriate and out-of-date 'doing things for them' approach. Social service organisations, to a greater extent than we often like to realise, become preoccupied with serving the needs of their own agencies, rather than those of the deprived. Backing is withheld from approaches which may hold the key to tackling poverty. It follows from our line of argument in this chapter that local authorities should accept a structure of decision-making and resource-distribution in which community action groups have a place as well as more conventional pressure groups.

Within the local authorities, there is little doubt of the increase in the number of social workers in the field who feel a strong identification with and a desire to support community action. The view was expressed amongst members of the sub-group that such workers could legitimately provide support for community action groups and could enable some struggling ones to continue. They could provide expert advice on where to find information, on how to obtain resources, on how best to approach the local authority. Some writers have also seen the statutory social or community worker in the role of advocate, taking the side of the local organisations or their members, putting their case before boards, tribunals and committees.

As has been frequently pointed out, the crunch for local authority employees comes when the community action groups take militant or public action against their authority. Social workers report that their superiors warn them not to side publicly with critical organisations, that they are expected to show deference to the assumptions of their employers; and hints are dropped that promotion prospects will be reduced. The radical social work journal *Case-Con* keeps a vigilant eye open for such cases but it seems that social workers' best means of protection in such circumstances stems from their own solidarity. In 1972 a significant step was taken when a large number of Islington social workers openly supported squatters. Open support is not the same as working with community action groups and it is fair to add that some activists are wary of local authority community workers, especially when their background and interests are so different from those of the deprived. They fear that such workers will manipulate local groups, perhaps in order to show evidence that they are getting things organised, and so may detract from the groups' original purposes.

Voluntary bodies   Both voluntary trusts and foundations and the large voluntary social work organisations have also viewed community action with some suspicion. The former are far more likely to put money into large-scale and relatively orthodox enterprises than to risk what may be much smaller sums on what is new and also more problematical. When a trust is asked for funds, it should be given a clear idea of the purposes of the group, as far as this is possible, although there are particular difficulties when policies may change drastically in view of changed circumstances. A group of tenants may come together with a particular purpose and find that all kinds of other issues need to be dealt with. What has to be avoided equally is *carte blanche* for those involved in community action whose vagueness may hide a confusion of purpose, and a rigid control which will not permit of experiment and changing priorities.

Other characteristics of trusts also serve to operate against the interests of community action. Like most other sources of support they tend to be disproportionately located in London and the southeast and hence tend to favour bodies already well equipped. They rarely take the initiative in encouraging small groups to apply but serve just those organisations well versed in the skills of money raising. They often favour demonstration projects into which money is put for a limited period of time. The demonstration project may suit the needs of research or publication but not those of community action groups which have no prospect of long-term existence without funds from outside sources. There is one trust which, in recent years, has become oriented towards community action, but this is at present the exception.

Traditional voluntary organisations tend to have little contact with community action groups although the large co-ordinating bodies are immersed in the field of community work. While there are exceptions, it is often considered that community action groups should not join councils of social service, for example, because this may affect the capacity of a council to obtain resources both from the local authority and from orthodox bodies such as Rotary Clubs etc.

Providing small amounts of money or a place to meet, or some help and advice in setting up a committee or structure, may be of far more use than actually being involved to a considerable extent in the activities of community action groups. In a few cases councils of social service have provided this kind of service, and in particular small amounts of money without strings, to help a group to overcome the basic problems which are particularly acute in the early stages.

Finally we ask: should community action be supported by the bodies to which we refer and should the development of community action groups be encouraged? The answer which we would give to this is that they *should* be encouraged, since the existence of groups able to bargain and act on their own behalf is as relevant to a pluralist society, and the British tradition, as it is to any radical or revolutionary models of society to which some of the community action groups might subscribe.

Recommendations

There are some recommendations which we think it would be helpful to make.

Information

More accounts of community action are needed. Bringing together existing accounts, from a great diversity of sources, would be desirable. These would be relevant to training and further study and to making public authorities and voluntary organisations aware of the kinds of initiatives taken by community action groups.

A handbook or guide is required, setting out questions and answers about how to operate as a group. (This could be used for the purposes of training, see below.) One purpose would be to make members of groups aware of the tactics commonly used to block direct action and campaigns at the local level.

Training

We think that some kinds of training are appropriate for members of community action groups and recommend that resources for training should be provided from public funds, so that those involved in community action can operate more effectively. There are precedents for this both in the USA and in the Northern Ireland Community Relations Commission. We are particularly concerned that groups should have the resources to organise training for their own members.

Finance

Nearly all public money is tied up in rather inflexible ways. We recommend that a proportion of the funds available for social development, whether central or local, should be allocated specifically to community action groups. Although the amounts may be small and there would of course be some risk involved in any unconditional financial support, nevertheless the benefits would be more than commensurate, both in the effective operation of the groups and in the greater flexibility of response by official bodies to social needs brought to their attention.

General

It is important to concentrate on developing the points of contact between official bodies—in particular local authorities—and community action groups, in order to familiarise those bodies with the aims and purposes of the groups. It is our hope that official bodies would then come better to recognise the contribution that community action groups have to make towards the establishment of a juster and more truly representative society.

5 Analysis and evaluation

Why analyse?

Is community work effective? By what criteria should it be judged? What works, at what levels, in what kind of situation? What efforts are doomed from the start to fail? What might ensure a measure of success? Questions like these may be asked from several points of view.

The first is that of the practitioner in the field. People who are engaged directly in community work need to know what has been effective or ineffective in the past, if they are to learn how to make their own work more effective and to avoid repeating mistakes. They need a set of criteria to judge their progress and a means of assessing the value of their work. Leaders and members of a local community, whether or not embarking upon community action, should also find useful guidance in the answers to these questions.

Teachers and trainers in community work similarly need a means of assessing projects which may then be used both as models for learning and for judging the work of students. Students themselves need to learn the techniques of evaluation as part of their training.

Organisations which initiate or support community work need some means of knowing what is worth while and what would be a waste of time. This applies to government departments and local authorities as much as to voluntary organisations and charitable trusts. Those who have to decide policy and how resources would best be used often lack clear-cut guidelines in assessing competing proposals; they too need to evaluate proposals and, later, their results.

Finally, the academic study of community work requires some consistent method of assessment. The theories underlying community work have received some attention already, but in a field of work so rapidly developing the continuation of such studies must depend on the interpretation of experience gained in the field. The task of communicating field experience to the theorist, and theories to the fieldworker, is complex and important. One essential tool is a recognised method of evaluating and interpreting material gained in the field.

Approach to a framework for analysis

For all these purposes, a framework for analysis is required. Such a framework need aim to do no more at this stage than to encourage consistency of reporting in community work. There must be room for personal interpretation and freedom for a variety of approaches to community work at different levels, but the patterns of information gained must be consistent with each other over a wide range of activity. This will enable a bank of comparable data to be established which could be available for practitioners and teachers, for research workers and theorists, and for policy-makers and innovators. The place for such a collection of information (suitably disguised should any problem of confidentiality arise) would be the resource centre discussed in chapter 8. Even without such a collection of comparable material, however, preliminary tests of the framework proposed suggest that its application to specific situations will be valuable on its own to those immediately concerned.

The problem of developing a framework for the analysis of community work could not be solved by taking any particular view of the nature of community work or of its objectives. People in many different situations, from the formal and hierarchical organisation to the spontaneous self-help group, become involved in community work, and the tasks they undertake vary. Practical and theoretical approaches have to be accommodated, with plenty of scope for the person using the framework to employ his own tools of understanding and interpretation. To exclude the personal viewpoint would be impossible and it could be argued that no analysis of community work would be complete without some subjective interpretation. It is important, however, to distinguish the subjective elements from the objective reporting, and to make clear the standpoint from which subjective observations are being made.

Besides allowing for different kinds of interpretation, a framework for analysis must take account of the notorious fluidity of community work. Time is the critical factor. Ideally a project will be monitored from its beginning (the point when the idea arises or the need is recognised) to an agreed point in time beyond that. It can then be evaluated at different points in time as it proceeds. An analysis can be made at any given point in time, with retrospective reporting and assessment of the earlier stages. This was in fact done in the test applications of the framework during its preparation. Above all, it is important to record events meticulously as they happen; memory is not a reliable guide.

However it is treated, the time factor is important. A project may show early signs of failure, but then succeed—or vice versa. People's roles and attitudes change over time. Posts and offices are held by different people. What is achieved may be different from what was intended: an effort to establish a council of social service, for example, may fail in that objective but it may be successful instead in establishing a different kind of group, or in changing the attitude of groups such as a local authority or deprived people in a community. Any framework for analysis must be applicable to any stage of a project. Ideally it will be applied several times, at key stages in the work.

There are other important variables. The roles people play affect their knowledge of a project, and their interpretation. While it must be clear who is doing any particular analysis and from what position, the framework for analysis itself should be capable of being used by anybody, within or outside the situation and with practical or theoretical interests. Similarly an analysis may be carried out for any one of several purposes and the same project may usefully be analysed by different people. The emphasis will be different for the fieldworker, for the theoretician, for the training institution, for the sponsoring organisation and for the grant-aiding body. There must be scope to accommodate the impact of events, such as a change of policy or power in the local authority, which are external to the project but may influence its progress. In other words a flexible, multi-dimensional, versatile tool is required: a framework to which can be applied the cladding which suits the situation, the people involved and the purpose of the analysis. To devise such a framework is not impossible: to apply it will still require skill and clear thinking.

The proposed framework for analysis

The framework consists of an introduction and three parts. The introduction sets the scene informally, identifies the analyst and defines the relationship of the analysis to the project in time. Sections 2 to 5 cover the planning stages. Sections 6 to 9 describe the events and the action. Section 10 links the events to the evaluation in Section 11. It is an opportunity for a subjective exposition of the factors below the surface of events: an x-ray, as it were, or infra-red picture of the hidden elements of personality, group dynamics, relationships and motives which are thought to have been significant.

The first attempt at a framework was tested by application to fourteen different projects in various parts of Britain. These were deliberately chosen for variety in their scope, their nature and their objectives. They included some projects on a large scale affecting an indeterminate number of people and some on a small scale involving, for example, the residents of one tenement block; projects involving new estates, established neighbourhoods and redevelopment areas; and projects concerned with general needs, with specific activities such as music teaching or co-operative purchasing and with processes such as the dissemination of information. The test applications, an example of which appears as Appendix 2, led to a number of changes in the construction of the framework but were essentially encouraging. The framework proved to be an appropriate structure for reporting and analysing community work projects: it works.

The Government Community Development Project and the Educational Priority Areas programme are both concerned with the evaluation of community work. Comparisons have shown that the development of a framework in the form presented here does not duplicate the work being done by these major government projects and indeed may prove useful to them.

None of those who have been involved in developing the framework would claim, however, that it is the only way of doing it or that it could not be refined and improved. It is presented merely as a first attempt, and a modest one, to suggest a way of carrying out an analysis. Further experience in applying it, and the ideas of others who have not yet been involved, will enable progress to be made. This is a beginning.

The framework can serve a variety of purposes. It can be used from any of the four points of view mentioned in the first section of this chapter and the information gained might differ according to the purpose for which it was required. Hence the importance of establishing, and stating, what the analysis is for. In preparing the framework, our attention was concentrated on field projects in community development, but it can be applied at any level and on any scale. The Government Urban Programme would be as appropriate a subject as the development of a playgroup. The more limited and defined the boundaries within which the framework is to be applied, the easier the task may prove to be, if only because of the amount of information which has to be collected; but analysis of the major schemes, partly because their scope and their objectives tend to be so elusive, may sometimes be the more worth while.

No special skills are necessary for the application of the framework. Intelligence and sensitivity on the part of the analyst will make the analysis more useful and more communicative. The help of a person outside the immediate situation under review, perhaps a social scientist, will combine the outsider's objective approach with the intimate knowledge of those engaged in the work to give the best results in many cases. The response to some of the sections would be enriched by a background of theoretical understanding or training in human relations but neither is essential to the framework's usefulness.

The framework need not be applied in full. Some sections will not apply to certain situations. The validity of an analysis will not depend on its completeness, but on the appropriate application of the relevant parts. For example, a trust considering whether to make a grant for a project may want to have sections 1 to 5 completed; or a fieldworker making an assessment of a community action project may find that there are no relevant organisations or policies and will therefore omit most of section 5. It may also be necessary to add sections for aspects not envisaged in the preparation of this framework.

The sketchiest of answers could be given to the questions raised. At the other extreme the work itself could be obstructed by the demands of over-elaborate evaluation. The depth and complexity of the analysis required will depend on the purpose for which it is being carried out and the judgment of those who are doing it.

The recording of data—events, plans, impressions, attitudes and so on—is of fundamental importance in producing a useful and effective analysis. There is no substitute for accurate information gathered at the time. Ideally, the recording of the planning stages would be complete by the time the work begins, and its progress should be recorded in some detail throughout its course so that the assessment will have a firm basis of fact.

The framework follows, together with some brief notes designed to make it comprehensible as a separate document. Appendix 1 provides an example of its application to an exercise in itself ludicrously simple, but helpful in illustrating the principles of application and the meaning of the terms used; while Appendix 2 is an example of one of the fourteen tests of the framework mentioned above.

The framework

The framework need not be applied in full. Any sections which are not appropriate should be omitted. Conversely it may occasionally be relevant to add something to the analysis which is not provided for in the framework.

The degree of detail in the assessment should be in accordance with the purpose for which the analysis is required.

The assessment may be made by an outside observer or by someone involved in the project. In the latter case the assistance of an outsider may be useful in counteracting unconscious bias. Any number of additional opinions may be given if this is thought useful.

The recording of data is fundamental to the success of the analysis. The work should be recorded in detail, from the beginning, at the time when each stage in its progress occurs, using the framework as a guide.

The work itself should not be allowed to suffer for the sake of the evaluation.

1 *Background*

General statement of the background and nature of the work undertaken	This section puts the work into context for readers who may not be familiar with it or with the areas where it is taking place. It should include a brief description

of the location and character of the area (if the work is based in an area), and of the broad social characteristics and prevailing attitudes of the people likely to be affected. In some cases a short history of developments leading to the present situation may be appropriate.

Brief statement on the person carrying out the analysis and the timing of the assessment

Who is carrying out the assessment and with what involvement in the work? At what stage is the assessment being carried out and what determined this? By whom is the assessment required and for what purpose?

2   *Reasons for the initiative*

The problem or situation as perceived by those initiating the work

Why was the initiative needed, how did the need come to be seen and how, if at all, was the extent of the need assessed?

Appreciation of the problem or situation by others

To what extent were the perceptions of the initiators shared by others, particularly those likely to be affected? The views of any outsiders would also be useful. 'Outsiders' in this context should be taken to mean people with some knowledge of the work but not actively involved in it. Mention should be made of any individuals or groups with a particular interest in the work in its planning stage.

3   *Objectives*

Definition—an objective is a specific aim relating to a particular situation, e.g. a greater proportion of small houses in a redevelopment scheme.

Objectives of those responsible for initiating the work, and of any others actively involved in planning it

Objectives may relate to tangible products or to relationships, attitudes or skills.

Priorities among the objectives and conflicts between them	It is possible that there may be neither priorities nor conflicts.
Means of measuring progress towards the objectives	This should say how it is proposed to evaluate the work against its objectives. There may be statistical indicators which should be mentioned. To what extent must measurement be subjective?

4 *Situation analysis*

An evaluation of the situation as it proved to be on examination when the work was beginning	This will complement section 1 and provide evidence of the situation and of the orientation of those involved in changing it. It will thus link with the process analysis of section 10.

5 *Organisation, policies and principles*

Organisation structures affecting the work, formal or informal	Examples might be a local authority housing department or a community action group. There may be several involved in the work. Diagrams or charts may be useful to illustrate them.
	N.B. This still refers to the planning stage. Organisations which become involved at a later stage will be mentioned in section 9.
External relationships of people chiefly involved in planning the work	Where these have not been mentioned under the previous heading—again, diagrams may be useful.
Existing policies affecting the work	*Definition*—a policy is an agreed statement of the means by which the objectives of a group might legitimately be achieved, e.g. to concentrate resources on providing branch libraries rather than a new central library, as a means of achieving the objective of bringing books within easy

reach of the greatest possible number of people. This section should also explain how the policies mentioned were decided upon and what are the attitudes of those planning the work to any of the policies which are not their own. Policies affecting the community itself rather than the work should not be included here but they may be relevant in section 2.

Principles guiding those responsible for the work

Definition—a principle is a general and fundamental guideline, e.g. an equal commitment to all of the people living in a particular area.

6   *Intended action*

Means of achieving objectives, i.e. methods by which those responsible plan to achieve their objectives

Definition—Methods might include large-scale measures such as the provision of a meeting place; also small-scale tactics such as taking minutes at a meeting.

Resources thought to be necessary: time and skills, total time scale, premises and equipment, funds

This need only be a brief statement.

Difficulties anticipated

This could cover any difficulties foreseen by those involved in planning, including any associated with concluding the work.

7   *Resources*

Resources marshalled at the beginning
    manpower—paid and
           voluntary,
        —full-time or
           part-time,
        —skills, training
           and interests,
        —external
           relationships
    premises and equipment
    funds

—if not mentioned under section 5

including sources

8 *Action*

Significant events

This section should give an idea of the character and progress of the work through a brief factual description of the most significant events, rather than a full narrative account.

9 *Development*

Changes in:
  resources—manpower
         —premises and
           equipment
         —funds
  roles of people involved or
  affected
  objectives
  policies
  principles
  methods
  organisation structure
  attitudes—of those
        responsible
        —of those affected
        —of outsiders

This section should identify and explain significant changes taking place as the work develops. It should say what was introduced, amended or rejected either deliberately or spontaneously, when the changes occurred and how and why they came about, i.e. how the work develops. Narrative should be avoided as far as possible by dealing with topics under the headings given. It might be relevant to say how the work was concluded and, for example, whether any of its functions were continued.

10 *Process analysis*

This section will vary greatly according to the work under review. It is intended to bring out any underlying factors which may not have been covered in section 9, particularly the influence of personality and group behaviour. The issues will be unquantifiable and the approach subjective. It may be appropriate to draw on theories of sociology and psychology.

11 *Evaluation*

Effects of the work
on the problem

This section should indicate to what extent those who planned the work and those doing it thought the problem described in section 2 had been alleviated by the time the evaluation date was reached.

Achievement of objectives	This should describe the extent to which the specific objectives mentioned in sections 3 and 9 were achieved at the evaluation date, according to the statistical indicators and any other criteria indicated in section 3.
Achievements outside the objectives	These may be additional to or instead of the achievement of what was intended in the first place.
Evaluation against resources	This should answer the questions: 'Were the resources adequate for the achievement of the objectives?' and 'Was the best use made of the resources available?' All resources mentioned in section 7 are relevant. Any hidden savings (e.g. reduced dependence on statutory social services) should be mentioned.
Implications for the future of the work	It may be useful to point out, for example, which objectives, policies and methods were altered, as described in section 9, as this could help others in planning their objectives and policies and deciding on their methods.
for other similar projects	What went contrary to plan, for better or for worse? The unexpected development is often the most instructive. Were there any key factors in the successful aspects of the work worth singling out?

Bibliography and supporting data

Sources of data for each section

Any other documents which would add to the reader's understanding of the project

Map of the area; note on the
methods of collecting data (with
copy of questionnaire, if used);
statistical data, e.g. balance   } if appropriate
sheet; extracts from diary of
events or descriptive report of
the work by someone involved.

6 Community workers and their employers

Fields of employment

A community worker, in the present context, is a person whose functions lie wholly or mainly in the practice of community work, as identified in chapter 1. The position of a member of parliament, or of a local authority, or a member of a board of management of a specialised service or industry is not discussed here; equally this chapter does not consider volunteers in community work, whether part-time or full-time. On occasion, it is these people who will decide whether the community work process succeeds or fails. They are excluded solely in order to focus attention on the community worker as a professional employee. At the end of the chapter and in the chapter on training, there is brief reference to the position of staff who may become concerned with community organisation, administration and planning, such as town planners and managers; also to that of teachers, doctors, caseworkers and others for whom community work may be a necessary but not a central activity. If they are excluded from the mainstream of the chapter, the importance of their function or of their potential contribution to community work is not thereby denied.

The community worker is a newcomer to the professions; and community work itself as a distinct activity is a recent arrival on the social scene in this country. Many of its leading exponents have indeed developed their interest through practical experience of community development overseas. The Association of Community Workers in the United Kingdom (ACW), founded in 1968, had 306 members at the end of 1972. Of these, 114 were employed by voluntary organisations, 125 by statutory bodies, 36 in education and training; the rest were either retired, students, not employed or in other kinds of jobs.*

How are we to identify the frontiers of community work sufficiently for the purposes of the present chapter or to distinguish from others those posts which are designed for community work properly speaking, or those which do in fact require community work training and practice? Clearly, it is the role and function of the worker, not the

* From information supplied by ACW.

title of his post, which is significant. There is one useful yardstick: is a particular post both designed and used primarily for work with (rather than for) the community? At first sight, the phrase *'with* the community' may not seem significant or helpful. But it points directly to the importance of the community worker's method and purposes and to his attitude to his task. It is not enough that his aims and activities should be in tune with community needs. What he does is indeed important; but *how* he sets about his task is of the essence of his function.

Descriptions of posts

In looking at the employment of community workers, it soon becomes clear that titles, descriptions and expressions used in advertisements of vacancies are diverse, and often ambiguous and inexact. Conditions of service are no less various and frequently inconsistent. The same title or description of a post may mean different things in the eyes of different employers. This is not surprising since many employing authorities with community responsibility or concern are acutely disturbed by the signs of malaise, division or even decay within local communities but have no clear idea of the remedies. They are content to encourage and support those whom they describe as community workers, in a process of diagnosis and experiment which they hope will bring a cure.

At the present stage of development it may often be advisable to give the skilled worker a free hand and a roving commission; and this is bound to be reflected in the language of advertisements and of job descriptions. As time goes on and experience accumulates, employers are likely to define the nature of the task more precisely. Even at this stage, however, special constraints or conditions and specific policies which an employer thinks essential are best set out clearly in the job description, so that the community worker knows when he accepts a position the limits within which he is expected to operate.

It is not easy to be precise when one tries to look behind the titles at the types of task for which community work posts are created. Some employing bodies have defined and limited purposes, in relation to which the workers' function stands out clearly. Others have a general responsibility for the development and well-being of communities and may seek to promote this by appointing staff with a variety of immediate assignments, some of them not apparently community work tasks at all. The administrative direction of the whole effort, which should set the tone and give the fieldworker the support he needs, is at present usually in the hands of senior officers for whom community work is not regarded as a central function: for instance, an executive head of a local authority, a director of social services or a chief education officer; or, in the voluntary field, a head of a social agency.

The employer may of course be either a statutory or a voluntary body. The distinction between the two relates both to the source of finance and to the auspices under which the work is done. The community worker in a voluntary organisation will find his prospects and continuity of employment governed by the source of finance. His salary may derive from year-to-year fund-raising, from a foundation project grant or from a local or central government subsidy for a fixed or indefinite term. The worker in a statutory authority on the other hand will have reasonable security of tenure and perhaps better career prospects. But he may be less free than the employee of a voluntary body to respond to the needs of the community according to his own unfettered judgment.

Even the worker in a voluntary organisation may be less independent than is often supposed. The financing authority may impose conditions or may hold the employing body and its staff to account if their activities incur too much criticism or hostility. Fortunately statutory authorities often recognise the advantages of using official funds to support voluntary effort—advantages which derive in part from the worker's freedom to experiment or to work with less inhibition than would be possible for the employee of a statutory body. Community workers in voluntary but grant-aided employment usually have a remarkably free hand in practice within the broad framework of a project, and this freedom may often be the unspoken intention of the financing authority. Voluntary bodies, such as the churches, which do not have access to public funds are not affected in this respect. But the scale of resources needed for effective intervention is likely to call in future for the injection of a proportion of public money into the majority of community projects.

A sample survey of advertised posts

The sub-group of the Community Work Group which discussed these questions needed more precise details about employment. The Gulbenkian Foundation therefore agreed to commission a sample survey of advertised posts for community workers in public and voluntary services. The survey embraced those posts which were advertised for England and Wales in five publications (*Guardian, New Society, Social Work Today* (fortnightly journal of the British Association of Social Workers), *The Times* and *The Times Educational Supplement*) during the twelve months ending 31 August 1971 and which carried a community work title or appeared to fall within the four headings in *Community Work and Social Change* (p. 149, section 1)*. 263 vacancies were identified covering 233 distinct posts. Further

* Community work includes: (a) helping local people to decide, plan and take action to meet their own needs with the help of available outside resources; (b) helping local services to become more effective, usable and accessible to those

details were sought through a questionnaire sent to prospective employers; 153 of these were returned and the responses are also embodied in the survey report (Ghazzali, 1972).

The survey was necessarily arbitrary: employers may or may not have advertised their community work vacancies; they may have advertised in other, more specialised or more local papers than those used in the survey; some posts listed may not in fact be concerned with community work while others may have escaped the author's drag-net. None the less the survey illustrates clearly the growing recognition by statutory and voluntary bodies alike of the need to employ community workers, and of the many opportunities open to trained people in this field during the twelve months covered by the survey. There is every sign that this trend has gathered momentum since that time.

Well over half of the 153 posts of which further details were provided by employers were newly created. It is also encouraging for the future prospects of community workers that 133 were permanent and only 20 temporary. As for the employing bodies, about six of every ten vacancies identified were advertised by a statutory authority, mostly for work in one of four local authority departments—education, housing, social services and planning. Local education authorities predominated, but anything up to half these posts, especially those in the youth and community service, did not seem to be designed for community work in the strict sense but for educational or group work or for the administration of a centre. Similarly some of the posts offered by social services departments primarily referred to casework or community care. In planning and housing departments there were several posts with interesting community work functions designed to encourage local communities to participate, in situations where there was little opportunity for this in earlier days. Not surprisingly, two other types of statutory authority appear in the list: new town corporations and the Community Relations Commission.

It has been said that, unless planners have direct contact with consumers and their needs, they are inevitably inclined to plan and design 'for themselves'. This happened in some degree in the early post-war new towns and the experience has underlined the need to ensure that social and community planning goes hand in hand with physical planning. It is here that the community worker has a partly prophylactic rather than a mainly remedial role. The social development officer of one of the more recently established new town

---

whose needs they are trying to meet; (c) taking account of the interrelation between different services in planning for people; (d) forecasting necessary adaptations to meet new social needs in constantly changing circumstances. Community work thus has in it aspects of direct neighbourhood work, closer relations between services and people, inter-agency co-ordination, and planning and policy formulation.

corporations has described the role of the corporation, and of his department within it, in these terms:

One can distinguish five major stages in the work of a corporation:
1. policy formulation;
2. structure planning of areas and services;
3. detailed planning of areas (including layout and design) and services;
4. implementation;
5. follow-through—when people are using whatever has been planned.

The recognised professions except for finance are concerned with some, but not all of these (e.g. planning with 2 and 3, quantity surveyor and architect with 3 and 4, housing with 3 and 5 and so on). Social development is concerned with them all. Our function is perhaps to ensure that whatever the corporation does is related to the people whom it will affect. As such we are the horses without blinkers, the professionals whose responsibility it is to see things as a whole instead of to contribute a particular part. This enables us to identify gaps in our activities as a corporation as well as to judge how people will in practice feel the cumulative effect of our various activities.

The other new field which is significant for community workers is in community relations, in areas of both immigrant and established communities, where differences in outlook or custom can easily lead to lack of mutual understanding and to discord. Here, as with community workers in new towns, the range of work is potentially wide, including the promotion of housing schemes, informal education, youth work and child care, as well as the encouragement of effective organs of community consultation and self-help.

The proposed integration of the three limbs of the national health service: general practice, the hospital service and the health services of local authorities (Department of Health and Social Security, 1972), is intended, among other purposes, to strengthen the health service in comprehensive community care. It should further hasten the provision of health centres and should enable the health services to reach the community more directly and effectively. The implications of this extended concept of community health remain to be fully explored. But it is clearly significant for the role and employment of community workers.

Under voluntary auspices, the two predominant employing bodies are councils of social service, particularly for work concerned with liaison between community groups, and community relations councils in urban areas with communities of differing cultures or backgrounds. In addition to these there is a great variety of independent bodies, many of them formed by citizens who are concerned to tackle some specific local need and have decided that they require skilled and experienced workers to help in meeting this. Much of the finance for these posts in voluntary agencies derives, as remarked earlier, from public funds.

Examples from the survey of advertised posts

A few quotations from the survey of the type of work proposed by an employer for a new or existing post should illuminate the subject. The following are from advertisements by statutory authorities:

Education authorities

' . . . assisting the community to identify its needs and mobilise its resources' (Hertfordshire);

' . . . developing links between the community and schools in the Home Office Community Development Project area of the city' (Coventry);

' . . . liaise with neighbourhood comprehensive schools and other local organisations to stimulate needs within the community' (Southampton);

'stimulating youth activity and harnessing the contribution of students to community work . . . encouraging relationships between the youth of the area and students' (Coventry, again).

Housing departments

'analysing of basic housing data and investigation into the changing pattern of living' (Birmingham);

'establishing of advice centres for housing improvement and developing citizen participation' (Liverpool).

Clerk's departments

' . . . action research. Developing the field of comprehensive social planning' (Glamorgan County Council);

'fostering the development and expansion of community services and participation' (Kirkby Urban District Council).

Social services departments

' . . . social planning, identification of community needs and research' (London Borough of Brent);

'assessing the needs of the locality and encouraging the community to meet more of its own needs' (Coventry).

Voluntary organisations used the following terms, among others, to explain the posts for which they were advertising during the survey period:

Councils of social service

'To encourage public participation in the replanning of the area' (Westminster);

' . . . promoting inter-agency co-operation in community work in the Borough' (Islington);

'encourage people to determine their social needs and priorities and help them to take collective action to improve their living conditions' (Northumberland and Tyneside).

Other organisations

'study and development of relations between the community and local schools'; 'assessing the needs of the local area in the field of community relations and acting as a source of advice' (Bolton Council for Community Relations);

'supervising five clubs for age groups under 5 to adult and an old people's day centre . . . exploring ways of intercommunication among these clubs and relating them to the whole community' (Sovereign Youth Club, Surrey);

'to investigate the relationship between the community and the organisation and content of community action schemes' (National Union of Students);

'Assisting in establishing the needs of a multi-racial community in a highly residential area' (Contact Centre, London);

'Initiation of survey research to determine the needs of young people in Earls Court' (Earls Court Experimental Work Project);

'To create a community within a new purpose-built block of flats' (YWCA);

'to . . . use community work, group work and family casework to overcome the problems of a deprived community' (Leicester Family Service Unit);

'Working with the Minister and local social services area team to discover and where possible to meet existing needs in the community' (Methodist Church, London Mission circuit);

'Working with adolescents of both sexes to bring about a more mature relationship between delinquents and the rest of the community' (Foxton Community Project).

The following identical job description for a community development project director (£3,366–£3,798) was published both by the *Education* Department of the West Riding County Council and by the *Social Services* Department of the London Borough of Newham: 'Assessment of human and material needs and problems of the area and to propose inter-service strategies for solution of problems.' This example offers a good illustration of the prevailing lack of frontiers in community work: initiative may come from a variety of directions, in this case from both education and social work. It is fortunate that employers are able at this stage to exercise exceptional freedom in deploying public resources from a variety of quarters to support new efforts to meet social needs.

We attempted to distinguish more precisely, among the posts listed in the survey, those which had as their primary task community work within the definition in *Community Work and Social Change* (quoted on pp. 80–1). For this purpose, two members of the sub-group studied the details given for the 233 posts in the survey. It is a measure of the difficulty of identifying the boundaries of community work that one member estimated that 60 per cent of the posts would fall within the definition, while the other thought only 10 per cent did so. In the present early stage of the development of community work, employers are apt to know less about the techniques of the work than their workers. Moreover it sometimes seemed doubtful whether the prospective employer understood the real needs of the community or was willing to find the resources likely to be needed by a worker. Did employers really appreciate what is meant by social change and the thinking behind the description of a community worker as 'an enabler, a catalyst, an adviser or an innovator of social change, according to the needs of a given situation'? (Gulbenkian Foundation, 1968, p. 35). Many employers seemed to think of the community worker as someone who, once employed and 'on the ground', would automatically resolve community stress or remove specific difficulties. Community work appeared also to be understood by some employers solely as a means for the co-ordination of services in deprived areas (rather than as a means of eliciting community participation), or to be regarded as a panacea for a social malaise which had defied conventional remedies. On the whole we do not think these uncertainties detract from the obvious community orientation of most of the posts concerned.

Descriptions of some posts specified work with a particular section of the community but did not suggest an integrative view of community needs and services. The tasks included work with the mentally and physically handicapped, drug addicts, young people, the aged and pre-school children. It would be quite inaccurate to suggest that the community worker is never specially concerned with one section of a local community, whether a particular age-group, those with a particular handicap or with a special need or concern (such as tenants), those affected by 'imposed' development plans, immigrants and so on. But his training would naturally lead him to see these special tasks in relation to the whole social situation of the local community. He might, for example, encourage local leaders to assume more community responsibility for groups in special need, or stimulate the community itself to establish and run an adventure playground or a pre-school playgroup. If the worker loses sight of the community orientation of his task, he is likely to find himself acting as a caseworker, a group worker, a teacher or an administrator. Although his task includes elements of all these, the distinction between his work and theirs lies in the way he sets about his assignment; in his relating a sectional need to the needs of the local community as a whole; and in his concern for the well-being and development of the whole community and of its component groups or sections in that context. A broad view of community work should encourage the development of an integrative approach by some of the specialists mentioned.

The examples of short job descriptions given on pp. 83–5 above show that employers were often thinking in terms of a well-defined community work assignment. Whether the worker succeeds in working effectively with a local community or whether he is led away into a more limited function, only a study of his work can reveal.

Prospects

Those who go into community work now have better opportunities and prospects as the scale and scope of community intervention increases. None the less there is still little career structure, except in related fields. Central government has only lately begun to recognise the separate existence of community workers. Local authority departments have yet to decide for themselves the level and terms of service for each community work post as well as fixing the salary ranges by reference to the Burnham, JNC, Soulbury and APT, etc. scales. In voluntary organisations, posts for fieldworkers differ widely in the nature of the tasks and the degree of responsibility; in community organisation there is a well-recognised structure for secretaries of councils of social service and other bodies with community work functions, but such posts are not numerous.

There are also new openings in community work teaching and research. Similarly, neighbourhood work is a valuable background for community organisation or community planning and administration. In these branches of community intervention, field experience is often a necessary qualification since practical knowledge is essential in getting to grips with the complexities of work with and between organisations or in planning a better community environment. So much for the survey of employment opportunities and the reflections to which it gave rise in the sub-group's discussions.

Problems of promotion within direct practice

The majority of recruits to community work are likely to be attracted into direct work with a local community, its individual people and its social groups. For some the next steps will be teaching, research, community organisation and community planning and administration. But it is to be hoped that some talented fieldworkers with skills tempered by experience and ability to inspire local leaders in times of stress will receive sufficient rewards in direct neighbourhood work. As community work develops and proves itself effective, more of such openings should be created, for instance, for senior workers able to give guidance to a field team, or for supervisors of a number of teams of community workers in a city with decaying inner areas. It would be unfortunate for the future of community work if those whose special abilities and inclinations continue to lie in direct work with communities were lost to fieldwork because of lack of prospects.

The role of other professions and the team

Many people other than community workers are concerned with community intervention. Some in social services, education, planning, health and other departments or agencies, are directly responsible for community projects and for community workers in the field. Others take a broad, community-based, view of their functions and grow into community work as they undertake senior duties, with a degree of responsibility for policy and planning. The executive head of a local authority in particular occupies a key position in setting the tone of the work and the services which his authority undertakes for, and to a growing extent with, the local community—a vital position of oversight and initiative, parallel with that held by the Home Office in relation to the Government Urban Programme. There are also signs that professions such as medicine, planning, architecture and education are starting to include a community orientation in their training and their perception of professional responsibilities. This aspect is further discussed in chapter 7 on training.

Although this study is about community workers, it should always be remembered, not least by the workers themselves, that they are part of a wider group of those whose functions affect the community. As such they depend in varying degrees on the support of public and voluntary services. Conversely, community workers' efforts must fit into the whole strategy of social improvement. In short, the community worker is part of a network of social intervention, even though he often has to operate as an individual or as one of a small group of individuals and may sometimes be in conflict with another service. A complex web of relationships is needed for effective co-operation. But common objectives cannot be assumed. Some can and should be defined in advance, while others will only evolve as work proceeds. In any event it is important that the individual workers and organisations concerned should be able to communicate with each other and should constantly do so. Without this, action based on individual assumptions will result in divergence of effort and in conflict. Increasingly, professional training stresses multi-disciplinary relationships in community work and elsewhere.

The community worker and the employing organisation

The community worker's activities reflect the purposes and specialised functions of the agency that employs him and should be based upon his best professional judgment. The influence of the employing agency on the general direction of its employees' work, although self-evident in practice, tends to be forgotten in the attempt to find a universal prescription for all workers. The worker is often discussed as though he were an autonomous practitioner, the constraints of his setting are under-estimated and the employing organisation tends to be seen as a distorting intrusion or an obstacle to appropriate action.

The Gulbenkian Study Group report pointed out (p. 65) that: 'statutory and voluntary organisations which employ community workers (or have members of their staff who devote part of their time to community work) do so as a means of carrying out the organisation's purposes . . . The purpose of the employing organisation sets limits to the kind of community work and has a strong influence on the direction it will take'.

The point is made even more strongly by Zald (1966, p. 56):

Indeed, much more of the variability of practice in community organisation is determined by its organisational context, as compared with many professional fields. The needs and problems of the community are not funnelled and defined directly between the practitioner and the community segment to which he is related; instead, needs are defined and shaped by the constitution and goals of the employing agency. Furthermore, the means selected to deal with community problems depend on organisational requirements, stances, and definitions. Whatever the practitioner's activity, he is guided by the structure, aims, and operating procedures of the organisation that pays the bills.

In practice, the purposes and assumptions of the agency and the worker are usually reconciled in varying degrees, but latent tension may remain. There may for instance be conflict of aims between improving existing services and social process directed to encouraging members of a local community to control their own destinies. The latter demands much time and energy, often with little apparent progress towards participation or effective action; and there are inevitably times when an employer needs to point to results as concrete achievements of his organisation or as justifying to his constituents the cost of employing the worker. There is always a tendency for the more motivated, the more able, the more upwardly aspiring people to take positions of leadership in a local community. If he needs to have something definite to show as the outcome of his efforts, whether it be the mounting of a demonstration or the organisation of a summer play scheme, the worker may be driven to relying on the more able and willing. The hard-to-reach will need far more help, and will need it for longer, if they are to participate; yet their participation may well be the key to success in the end. In short, tensions between task and process orientation can bring workers into conflict with their employing agency, particularly if the agency is under pressure to produce demonstrable results. (For a case history of these and related issues see Mitton and Morrison, 1972.)

Community groups and social action

The more successful the efforts of a community worker, the more likely it is that a community group will take on a life of its own. Indeed this is the purpose of his work. But the group may then take the bit between its teeth and embark on something which the employing agency considers beyond its scope, irrelevant, or even objectionable. Once it is capable of self-direction, the community group may raise awkward questions or bring pressure to bear on the agency itself and this can place the worker in a difficult position. Yet given goodwill and competence on the part of both worker and agency, and given that the agency embarked on the work with its eyes open, with a genuine desire for their autonomy and determined to overcome any consequent difficulties, it should usually be possible to avoid direct conflict between such groups and the agency employing the worker. A more difficult situation arises when a group acts against other organisations with which the employing agency has important relations in terms of authority and resources, for instance another department of the same local authority or a voluntary agency in relations with a local authority. Here again, it should be possible to settle matters, if the two organisations are determined to give the greatest possible weight to community viewpoints.

It would be well to recognise at this point that community workers may sometimes exert undue influence. They may at times be incompetent or irresponsible or may unconsciously seek to further their own aspirations or emotional needs, rather than those of the groups they are supposed to serve. Good standards of training and practice will reduce the risk of this. None the less there remain valid questions about the relationship between worker and community group. It is too naive to argue that the worker is only an enabler and facilitator of group processes; that he attempts to create the conditions for informed and effective action; but that the decisions are made by the group without intervention by him. Whether he wishes to or not, the worker will to some extent be exercising an educational role; he will be influencing the group's understanding of its situation and the action it takes in many different ways, not least by working with it at all. He cannot therefore escape some responsibility for the decisions which the group makes. Clearly the influence that a worker should properly exert varies in different circumstances. In working with disorganised, apathetic and deprived populations, a more supportive and active role may be required if the worker is to be of real help to the group, at least in the initial stages, than would be appropriate for groups with greater social skills and resources. There is often a fine distinction between a degree of legitimate and necessary leadership and the improper and destructive manipulation of a group.

Since the community worker may have this power to exert undue influence and to undermine the self-direction of a group, he needs a disciplined awareness of what he is doing and the capacity to direct and control his own influence in the interests of the group's development; here again the importance of a thorough understanding of the educational and other processes at work in the group is obvious. But the dangers of the situation should not be overemphasised: groups are not unresisting material to be moulded at will. While the worker is usually armed with little in the way of rewards or sanctions in his dealings with groups, they have many ways of overtly or covertly determining their own direction. Although for the worker difficult issues of principle may be involved, the employing agency and the wider public may think that he is not controlling his constituency enough, or in the direction desired by the critic.

Community workers and elected representatives

It is sometimes feared that the community worker may usurp or threaten the role of the elected members of a local authority. The worker's role is, in principle, quite distinct from that of an elected representative and his objectives, methods and position in the community are different. But in practice a number of factors tend to confuse the issue:

some councillors may be involved in activities very similar to those of community workers;

some people involved in community activities, even calling themselves community workers, are essentially political activists;

a number of issues which confront community groups and community workers are in essence political although not necessarily party issues;

the councillor very often carries a dual role as a representative who is also responsible for decisions and services which community groups may be contesting;

if the community worker is employed by a local authority, the councillor is a member of the employing body.

In helping local groups to articulate their needs and press forward towards their objectives, a community worker may well be seen as a potential rival to a councillor. Community groups may sometimes be in conflict with councillors but this is not intrinsically improper or subversive. There are signs that more councillors are coming to realise that both community groups and workers can be a valuable resource and are taking the initiative in encouraging community groups and in appointing community workers. One of the purposes of studies such as those undertaken as part of the Government Community Development Project (CDP) is to discover in what conditions the relationship between community workers and local councillors can be creative. There are now numerous examples of harmonious co-operation between local councillors and the CDP teams. In more than one area they are working side by side in such a way as to supplement rather than to supplant the normal channels of communication.

The opportunities and constraints of organisation

Clearly the character of an organisation, its resources, its power, its responsibilities and its relations with other bodies help to determine and delimit the objectives of its workers. This influence may be constructive or destructive, providing both opportunities and constraints, whether the organisation works within or outside the system. The opportunities and benefits of organisation are obvious, and resources in money, facilities, information, expertise or influence are indeed vital to the success of community groups and workers. Without organisation, work with community groups would be left to the autonomous volunteer.

The constraints which organisation brings with it tend to be more obtrusive than the benefits. They may seem to arise from structural defects or from rigidity, insensibility, incompetence, inertia or self-interest. Decisions and practices which a worker feels restrict his efforts with particular groups may arise from his employer's attempt to fulfil other equally valid purposes. Pursuing issues of primary importance to one group may endanger resources and arrangements of primary importance to other groups and individuals, to whom the organisation has a commitment. If he is mainly involved with one group or with a number of groups whose needs are not competitive, the worker is not himself torn in two directions; but if he is engaged with groups making competitive or contradictory demands, the dilemma confronts him directly. For example, a worker assisting a residents' group, one of whose main demands is to get rid of the problem families or vagrants or unsupported mothers who live in the neighbourhood might also be charged with supporting the latter and helping to integrate them within the local community.

Among the factors which determine the extent of possible conflict between a worker and his employing organisation are:

the extent to which the organisation has a variety of purposes or one single objective: the more diverse the purposes of the agency, the greater the risk that the concerns of a particular worker or group will conflict with other purposes, equally desirable from the standpoint of the organisation;

the degree to which an organisation exposed to conflicting demands has the resources to cope with them;

the degree of ideological commitment: organisations with a clear and specific basis of values, assumptions and purposes are likely to attract and select workers who share their beliefs. If conflict arises between the aims of the organisation and the aims of the client group, the worker is then likely to decide that it is the group rather than the organisation whose attitudes need to be changed;

the extent to which the organisation is dependent on outside sponsors for the resources it needs to fulfil its purposes; the more vital to the purposes of the organisation are those resources, the more reluctant it will be to enter into conflict with its sponsors, whether public or private.

But it is not necessarily in the best interest of the community group to gloss over or avoid such conflicts at all costs. Sometimes the worker's freedom of action is vital to the success of the group. In other situations this freedom may be preserved at the expense of any effective progress by the group towards meeting its needs.

Some further distinctions can be made in relation to the three broad categories of employing organisation—statutory, voluntary and community group.

In statutory organisations

The existence of constraints in statutory bodies is self-evident and needs no elaboration. Their legal basis, public accountability, hierarchical structure and democratic control limit the nature and extent of their relations with sectional community groups. This is not to imply that the limits will necessarily be reached or that any initiative is therefore pointless. On the contrary, statutory services of various kinds are so valuable to individuals and groups that official bodies are bound to be directly involved with community groups despite the difficulties. These limits are neither as narrow nor as rigid as is frequently assumed. Some statutory bodies are, in fact, engaged in direct work with community groups which is as enterprising and productive as much of what is being done under non-statutory auspices. Unfortunately it is in those areas where public anxiety is liable to be aroused, because of activities which upset some members of the local community, that there is the greatest need for such joint endeavour.

In voluntary organisations

Voluntary bodies by contrast are generally regarded as more responsive and invested with greater freedom of action. It is true that they do not labour under the same constraints of public accountability. Statutory bodies may recognise this and support work with community groups by grant-aiding voluntary organisations in situations where direct support might be controversial. Moreover groups suspicious of, or hostile to, statutory authority may find it easier to accept the interest of a voluntary body; and the community worker may have greater freedom of action at one remove from the ultimate paymaster. Yet, as already indicated, where the statutory body provides the funds, it can powerfully influence the voluntary body if it chooses to do so. The latter may indeed 'over-restrain' its enterprise for fear of losing official support by initiatives which attract unwelcome publicity or cause official embarrassment.

Even if a voluntary organisation is independent of statutory support, its sources of funds will affect its policies. For instance, if it is a membership organisation it will probably not become heavily involved in work with outside groups, unless they are likely to become members; and the members are likely to have fairly clear-cut expectations of the staff. More often voluntary bodies rely on outside subscribers, usually a more amorphous constituency than members and less likely to have specific aims. Nevertheless, the initiatives of such a voluntary body will be influenced by what will attract or repel subscribers. But voluntary bodies are seldom in a position to fund any substantial work with community groups solely from voluntary sources, and have to rely mainly on public or trust funds. It is to be hoped that grants in this field will in future have few strings or other constraints attached.

In community groups

Direct employment by community groups seems to offer an attractive solution to the conflicts of loyalty and responsibility which can upset the worker. The third party disappears, community group and employer are one, and the worker's accountability is clear. But the groups most in need of the services of a community worker are extremely unlikely to be able to support him from their own resources. In the initial stages they may be able to obtain funds from voluntary sources but in the long run they will probably have to rely on statutory support, which has the implications already discussed. Few groups need a full-time community worker or are able to obtain the resources to employ him. A number of them would thus have to come together in some form of federation. This would begin to re-create the community group-worker-employing organisation triangle, particularly when new groups came into an established federation at later stages.

In practice few community workers—not even those most vocal about being solely responsible to the community—are directly employed by community groups; and some who have experience of this have not been altogether happy. For example, a worker may feel almost too clearly and too closely accountable to the employer and even more vulnerable to pressure against his own best judgment than in the conventional employment situation; while he may be acting under the direction of the group, he may not think he is acting in their best interests. He may also feel a responsibility towards other groups whose interests are being ignored or overridden by his employing committee, so that conflicts of responsibility arise. This is inevitable when community workers have not yet made good a claim to exercise a professional judgment which is binding on them and their employers.

The dilemmas of the community work role

As has already been indicated, over a wide range of work there are no inherent difficulties; and some difficulties are as much dilemmas of practice as of sponsorship. But there are some community workers who have difficulties with their employing agencies and operate under constraints which they feel are not in the interests of the groups with which they are working. Critical problems arise when community action turns into conflict with the wider community, on which the agency and the worker are dependent for their support.

As has been said above, these situations are particularly likely to arise in relation to socially deprived groups when activity of which other segments of the local community may disapprove becomes all the more evident as a result of community work.

In public authorities and voluntary services of various kinds it seems that beyond a certain point the worker's role moves from being primarily professional to primarily political. Since there is a political element in much community work, there are no clear guidelines for judgment. This depends on the nature or level of the issues at stake and the remedies being advocated; on the kind of activity involved and who is undertaking it; on its relation to party political activity and on the attitudes and policies of those who control the resources upon which the employing organisation is dependent. Community workers, whether or not they regard themselves as having political roles, cannot escape political situations. This creates difficult questions for both professional and employing interests. How far should, or could, community workers be selected and trained to undertake what are essentially quasi-political roles? They can hardly be expected to develop both the skill and the judgment needed to influence policy by political means and, at the same time, the open-ended relationships on which their effectiveness depends.

Contradictions and strains can usually be handled or lessened if the issues are openly faced at an early stage and the scope and limits of action for the community group, the community worker and the employing organisation made clear. Misunderstandings and unproductive conflict may be minimised by stating clearly what policies and what limits must be accepted if a community group is to receive staff assistance and other resources. Otherwise the worker remains in an ambiguous position in which neither he nor the group with which he is working know where they stand in relation to the employer. For their part, employing authorities do well to ensure that community workers are fully consulted when policy options are being formulated and reviewed. If viewpoints are clarified or modified in committee rather than in public, potentially disruptive issues can usually be settled without impairing joint community effort. If differences of approach are in fact so fundamental as to be irreconcilable, there are obvious advantages in bringing them to light at an early stage rather than as a result of a breakdown in a community development project. Fortunately the constraints that are put upon their workers differ considerably in nature and extent from one employer to another; it follows that the more varied are the sponsoring organisations, the more flexible are likely to be the services available to community groups.

Co-ordinating work between organisations

Many of the issues that have been considered also concern community workers at the inter-organisational level. These relate first to the consequences for the people concerned of the activities of such workers and second to the problems of inter-organisational action in itself.

For those who work at this level, the people in a local community are distant, so that insufficient weight may be given to their views. While those who work with community groups may sometimes tend to make unreasonable demands on their own or other agencies, the inter-organisational worker may be too reluctant to bend structural or administrative patterns to fit the changing needs of people. The Skeffington Committee commented (1969, para. 2): 'In a large, complex and socially advanced industrial nation like ours ... the principle of public participation can improve the quality of decisions by public authorities and give personal satisfaction to those affected by the decisions.' Many services have increasingly come to realise this and have appointed staff with a special responsibility for relating the organisation more effectively to those whom it exists to serve.

Community workers employed by an individual service agency are in a different position from those employed by a co-ordinating organisation. In the former case, the employing body is itself an interested party, while in the latter, it is neutral. In practice one and the same organisation may be protagonist in one context and co-ordinator in another.

In a service organisation

The focus here is on agencies which exist to provide services or resources to meet human need, a wide range of statutory or voluntary organisations of which a local authority social services or social work department is a good example. Such bodies cannot but develop relations with other organisations which can help or hinder them in their task and often need resources which are controlled or influenced by other bodies if they are to offer a comprehensive service to individuals or communities in need. Increasingly, organisations have come to acknowledge this wider responsibility.

In 1965 Donnison wrote (p. 248):

Chief officers are responsible for the agencies they direct, but our studies show that some of the social services' most important tasks are performed by staff in several different agencies . . . Fruitful development of the work calls for the participation of many people outside the agency, and a willingness to subordinate the interests of the agency to those of the people to be served; otherwise the evolution of social policies may be frustrated or wastefully distorted.

It may be admitted here that such an outward-looking, 'anti-bureaucratic' attitude is the more difficult for members of a large organisation to maintain, the larger it becomes. How much easier and more comfortable is the protective closing of ranks with which people in large organisations may often be tempted to confront criticism.

A community worker who is specially responsible to his service agency for promoting joint action with other bodies is naturally identified by them with his own employer. Yet he may at times feel called upon to advocate policies which are more acceptable to those other bodies than to his own agency. For example, a preventive approach to the needs which a social services department or agency exists to meet might logically lead to developing housing or education services, perhaps at the expense of further expansion in the social services in a stricter sense. A community worker in this position might easily be unable to reconcile his own diagnosis of the needs and his judgment of the priorities with the existing policy of his employing agency or department, however welcome his opinion might be to some of the other bodies with whom he had dealings. Conversely, he might feel called upon to criticise the policies or practices of those other bodies to an extent which could endanger their good relations with his department.

In these situations, the outcome is likely to depend on whether the community worker succeds in convincing his employer that his views are justified or whether on the other hand the employing agency decides to restrict his freedom of action in the interests of its existing policy or its good name with related organisations. Such dilemmas of the community work role may appear obvious when stated but need, nevertheless, to be mentioned, if the worker's position as a professional person and as an employee is to be clearly appreciated.

In a co-ordinating organisation

In the case of an employing body engaged in a joint activity, such as a local authority clerk's or planning department or a regional or national agency, statutory or voluntary, the potential for conflict is clear. As in 'grass roots' work, the people who are affected by the work being done may take a different view of the situation from that of the employing body, while having little, if any, influence over it. From this arises a risk of conflict between the employing body and the participating organisations and of divided loyalties for the community worker. In theory this situation disappears when he is employed by a joint or multi-purpose organisation embodying the agencies whose co-operation he is charged to promote, such as a council of social service or a new town corporation. But even then, the latent issues persist as between the worker and those with whom he is working, who are both employer and clientele. His assessment of the situation may well differ from that of some or all of the participating bodies and, in a sense, this could justify his employment. The worker's actions in relation to particular issues may therefore be inhibited or directed by his position in relation to his employers.

Local or segmental co-ordination

Particularly intractable problems of practice arise in relation to efforts at co-ordination and joint action at lower levels or by organisations within a hierarchy and the worker's employment position is a relevant factor here. By definition, inter-organisational work attempts to bring together the activities of independent or relatively independent organisations. But the organisations may well be subject to more or less compelling influences from outside; their policies and activities may not be determined locally; they may be branches of national organisations, some of which are highly centralised; or they may be affiliated to national associations which influence their work. Local offices of statutory bodies may be part of a local authority or of central government departments. While many of these 'external' influences can be positive, they limit the freedom of action of more local bodies. The horizontal lines of communication and action will usually be weaker than the vertical lines and this creates major barriers to co-ordination and joint planning.

The worker who is promoting joint action may find that this conflicts with policies at higher levels, both in the organisations with which he is working and in his own. He may find himself precluded from pursuing certain lines of action for reasons unrelated to the matters in question. The issues are likely to be particularly acute in relation to the various types of 'priority area' and 'positive discrimination' which have been advocated for housing, education, social services etc. The Seebohm Committee, for example, was convinced (1968, para. 487) 'that designated areas of special need should receive extra resources comprehensively planned in co-operation with services both central and local, concerned with health, education, housing and other social needs'. The need here is both to concert the efforts of separate organisations and at the same time to shift the allocation of resources. The political and administrative base for this is weak and as the Seebohm Committee points out (para. 490): 'The political, administrative and professional problems associated with securing truly comprehensive planning between local authority departments and other organisations concerned with such development areas are likely to be formidable and need special study.' Particular interest in this connection attaches to the Government CDP; an attempt, through the close co-ordination of central and local, official and unofficial effort, to tackle social needs comprehensively in the older urban areas. Experience here should be closely scrutinised. If the 'grass roots' community worker may threaten the role of the elected councillor this can also happen at inter-organisational level. Here the worker is involving his own organisation in joint enterprises with other bodies which may well have policy implications for the elected councillor. In practice the difficulties do not seem to cause much anxiety and merge with more general questions of the respective roles of elected members and full-time officials.

The dilemmas of the worker at the inter-organisational level in relation to his employing body do not seem usually to give rise to acute problems. By its very nature inter-organisational work is less obviously focused on a particular worker. Questions of relationships with other bodies are part of the whole work of the organisation. In both statutory and voluntary agencies people at many different levels may play a part in this work. Committee members, particularly the chairman, the director or chief officer, senior administrative and professional staff and the staff in the field, will be involved in varying degrees. At this level too, there are conventions and procedures for managing inter-organisational problems. There may be a fund of greater sophistication and skill and more experience of handling situations as they arise. For much of the time inter-organisational work is also a great deal less public than 'grass roots' work. The type of action by community groups discussed in chapter 4 is, by contrast, a new phenomenon which cuts across existing assumptions and has still to be established as a normal part of the social scene.

There may, however, be less comforting reasons for the apparent lack of serious problems at this level. One possibility is that the needs of those ultimately affected by inter-organisational work are too often disregarded. The needs of organisation and the desire for harmony and compromise between various bodies may come to take precedence. Or the comparative lack of concern about the role of the worker at this level might reflect the lack of effective action. Constraints and limitations are perhaps too readily accepted. Yet the Social Work (Scotland) Act 1968 states in Section 12: 'It shall be the duty of every local authority to promote social welfare', while the Seebohm report (Recommendation 120, p. 230) said that: 'Effective co-ordination with other services and individuals, and the mobilisation of community resources to meet need are aspects of the administration of the social service department, as important as its internal management and demanding as much skill.'

The same aims of internal and inter-agency co-ordination, of interdisciplinary action and the mobilisation of community resources apply also to other services. If these obligations are accepted it is likely that the activities of workers at inter-organisational level will become more controversial in the future than they have been in the past, largely because of the sheer rapidity of social change and thus the pressure for flexibility and advance in the social services, compared with relatively static situations in the past.

Community work as a subsidiary task

In this discussion, 'work with community groups' and 'inter-organisational work' have each been dealt with in relative isolation as a 'thing
in itself'. In practice the broad categories of work with community
groups and inter-organisational work cover a very wide range of
activity; and some of the latter is primarily a matter of administrative
skill in a large organisation. In any event the categories overlap and
are interrelated. Both are aspects of community interaction although
directed to different targets. Both have assumptions and considerations in common and neither is adequate without the other.

For many people, however, a community orientation is a necessary
element in their work though not its primary purpose—for example,
for general practitioners, health visitors, lawyers, teachers, caseworkers, administrators, housing managers, planners. Expertise,
seniority and a well-established major role may sometimes place
those for whom a community orientation is incidental in a more
favourable position than the full-time worker. There are also disadvantages. The major role of other professions may give their
practitioners insufficient time for the community aspect. Moreover,
they may well not have enough opportunity to develop the skill and
experience required for effective community work. Specific professional interests may obscure other relevant aspects of the situation.
Beyond this, the primary professional task may be an obstacle to
gaining the confidence of individuals or organisations. The responsibilities of these other professions, while they give scope and
discretion in matters clearly within that field, may prevent their
practitioners from moving into areas outside their particular fields,
even if this is what the situation demands.

Conclusions

1   It is important that many people in the public service, the helping
professions and voluntary service should have a specific community
orientation in their work. Many who are not appointed primarily as
community workers will be directly engaged in community work to
some extent and this is highly desirable. Nevertheless there is a need
for people whose primary job is community work, at the 'grass roots',
in community organisation or in community planning and administration. More such appointments are being made and this is to be
encouraged.

2   The location of community work in local government will vary:
social services or social work, education, planning and other departments will all bear substantial responsibilities. Several departments
are bound to be concerned in each local authority, to an extent which
may vary according to the local situation and the attitudes of elected

members or officials. Among the theoretical options would be, first that community work should be identified as mainly a function of social services or social work departments; second that this function should be allocated to all the chief officers responsible for education, social services, planning, housing and so on, with the chief executive officer of the authority as co-ordinator; and third that the latter's deputy should be designated as specially responsible for community interests, so that he could direct and co-ordinate community services, without the creation of a new department. The concept of corporate management, to be introduced in the reorganisation of local government in 1974, should make it easier to secure departmental and political co-ordination, in the interests of a concerted community work approach. The local authority associations may wish to clarify some of the issues for their constituents in a matter which involves complex issues of power and authority, to which there is not necessarily a single solution.

3   At the 'grass roots' the most delicate issues arise when workers, particularly those employed by public authorities, become involved in the more unconventional and militant forms of community action. Workers at the inter-organisational level seem less likely to find themselves at variance with their employing bodies and this may sometimes reflect a lack of effectiveness.

4   In principle there is no difficulty in distinguishing the roles of community worker and elected representative in local government, but in practice the distinction may be less clear-cut. The problem becomes acute when workers employed by a local authority are involved with groups and organisations in conflict with that authority, and so with those of its members who are committed to the policy of the authority.

5   Tensions between the community worker and his employing organisation cannot be eradicated, for they spring from the nature of the task; but conflict can often be minimised and managed. Possible approaches include the following:

organisations should attempt to develop increased understanding of community work and sufficient flexibility to enable it to be practised effectively;

community workers should stimulate greater understanding and support for their role within their own employing organisation;

training for both employers and workers should give greater attention to the organisational settings in which community work is practised;

every effort should be made to increase public understanding of community work;

employers should clarify their objectives so that difficulties may be avoided or anticipated. Workers should be involved in policy formulation.

6 In view of the potential constraints of any employing organisation, community work should not be seen as the exclusive province of any one body or service. It is in the public interest to have a variety of employers, both statutory and voluntary.

7 In order to attract and retain workers a more adequate career structure should be developed. In particular, means should be found of promoting community workers within field practice, rather than accepting that the only avenues of promotion are through administration or teaching.

8 Restrictive professionalism is undesirable in this field. Professional standards are necessary in the positive sense of:

an ability to offer skilled and appropriate help;

a commitment to certain values concerned with human worth and dignity;

action in the interests of the community rather than the professional worker's own interests or those of others extraneous to the situation;

a measure of autonomy and self-direction, so that the professional worker is not merely the creature of his employing organisation or community group but is able to take a wider perspective and act according to his best professional judgment.

Such professional standards should provide safeguards for the worker, the groups and organisations with which he is working, his employer and the community as a whole.

7 Training

In this chapter we are concerned with educational and training processes for many different kinds of people. This discussion of training starts where part 3 of the Gulbenkian Study Group report left off. That framework and general assumptions are not discussed again but we have attempted to discover what changes in thought and action there have been in the past five years, whether leading to a clearer pattern and more general training for community activities, or to greater chaos; what there is fresh that can usefully be said, and what previous findings seem to be contradicted or confirmed; still valid or overtaken by change.

The earlier Study Group report classified those who needed systematic community studies or training in some form into:

full-time community workers at different levels;

those for whom it would be part of their total training and practice, for example caseworkers, youth workers, the clergy and some educators (e.g. in informal adult education); and

those who need an intelligent understanding of community processes in the course of their work, notably planners, architects, general practitioners and community psychiatrists, health visitors, educators in general, administrators, lawyers, the police, volunteers in community work and others active in it on their own behalf.

This framework will continue to be used in the present chapter.

The following changes, amongst others in the field of training, have taken place since the Study Group report was published:

the three separate training councils for the child care, health and welfare and probation and after care services have been amalgamated in the Central Council for Education and Training in Social Work (CCETSW) which covers the United Kingdom. The promotion of training for community work is specifically mentioned as part of the new Council's responsibilities;

in the place of the one-year youth service course at the National
College for the Training of Youth Leaders there are now six
courses in youth and community work in various educational
institutions in England; these include the separate courses for
youth leaders and community centre wardens at Westhill College
which have been integrated into one course for youth and
community workers. There are also four such courses in Scotland.
These courses are under the auspices of the area training
organisations of university institutes of education in England
and Wales and of the Standing Consultative Council on Youth and
Community Service in Scotland;

specialised courses in community work have been started at the
University of York and University College, Swansea (the latter
is a stream within the applied social studies course);

the community development courses in the adult education
departments of Edinburgh and Manchester Universities have been
more specifically directed to students who will practise in this
country, as well as those intending to work overseas;

an option in community work has been started in the M.Phil. at
York University, in the diploma in social work studies course
at the London School of Economics and in several other university
courses in social work;

the National Institute for Social Work Training has developed
closely related theoretical teaching and fieldwork, based upon
its Southwark Community Project, for students taking the
community work option in its one-year course for qualified and
experienced social workers;

there is a marked increase in the teaching of community work
and in related fieldwork in social work training;

many colleges of education are including in teacher training
more courses about the local community and the social services
and several now provide options with a family and community
bent; and

there is an increasing number of part-time two- or three-year
courses in community work leading to a certificate or diploma.
These are designed primarily for practising community workers or
as 'conversion' courses for youth workers, caseworkers, teachers
and others. Examples are the three-year part-time day release
certificate course at the University of Leicester which comprises
30 weeks' work a year including fieldwork on one day each week
in the second and third year, a part-time course at the Polytechnic
of North East London and two-year day release courses leading

to a diploma or certificate in social studies at the Liverpool University Institute of Extension Studies. A two-year post-graduate CNAA (Council for National Academic Awards) diploma course is at the planning stage at the Birmingham Polytechnic. Other part-time courses may also have some community work content.

It is clear also that many more administrative and professional groups are taking account of what they consider to be the 'social dimension' of their work. The setting up of the Civil Service College and the establishment of the Institute for Local Government Studies at Birmingham University have both stimulated the training of public administrators in social studies. The Home Office has, through its own and other training programmes, encouraged a greater social awareness in those who work in the police and in the prison service. Recent developments in the curricula of medical and para-medical training and of training for planners, architects and others (referred to in more detail below), all indicate a growing recognition of the need to understand more about the communities with which these professions are involved.

The earlier Study Group, reporting in 1968, foresaw a danger (p. 147) that 'community work may soon become so fashionable that educational institutions will be encouraged to establish training courses with inadequate facilities for theoretical teaching and field practice. To avert this danger, education and training in this field should at first be concentrated in a few university or other educational institutions in two or three areas. They should be able to depend largely on local resources, particularly in fieldwork.'

An attempt to assess present developments

In order to get as much information as possible about current thinking and action related to training for community work, written material was collected from various sources with the help of government departments, educational institutions, professional associations, voluntary organisations and individuals. In particular an attempt was made early in 1972 to bring up to date the information collected for the original Study Group in 1967. A letter asking for information about the current teaching of community work was sent to forty-two departments in universities and polytechnics affiliated to the Joint University Council for Social and Public Administration (JUC) and to forty-four other courses recognised by the CCETSW, whether in university extra-mural departments, polytechnics, colleges of further education or colleges of education. A similar letter was sent to those in charge of seven courses in youth and community work and to certain university departments of adult education with courses in community development. Replies were received from thirty-four JUC members (excluding Manchester Polytechnic, already counted under

youth and community work courses); twenty-three other courses
recognised by the CCETSW, seven youth and community work courses,
three adult education departments with courses in community development and Birmingham Polytechnic with a Council for National
Academic Awards degree in sociology which includes an option in
community work. An analysis of the material received from these
institutions appears in Appendix 3, and the detailed content of some
community work courses in Appendix 4.

Comments on information sent by a number of educational institutions

Changes in thought and action over the last five years may be said
from the replies received to the enquiry to have been four-fold:

> First, there has been a substantial increase in the number of
> institutions providing courses that include teaching and fieldwork
> placements in community work. In some instances the extent
> of teaching is limited but, bearing this in mind, at least
> twenty-six members of the JUC now provide courses. Not less
> than twenty other educational institutions with social work
> courses recognised by the CCETSW provide some teaching; together
> with three university adult education departments; one polytechnic;
> and seven institutions offering what are now entitled youth and
> community work courses. One of the latter takes the expanded
> title to imply helping the students to understand the communities
> in which they live, to see how their work with young people can
> relate to this and to understanding the skills and approaches used
> by other community workers and how these can overlap with
> their own.

> In the second place, eleven of the courses included above (other
> than those in youth and community work) are specifically in,
> or have separate options or streams in, community work. These
> courses are provided by the Universities of Belfast, Exeter,
> Glasgow, Manchester and York; University College, Swansea; the
> London School of Economics; the Polytechnics of Birmingham,
> Hatfield and Teesside, and the National Institute for Social
> Work Training. At York University there is now both a Reader and
> a Lecturer in Community Work on the staff.

> Third, there is marked interest expressed by staff who would like
> to include teaching in community work in existing courses
> if time allowed, or if fieldwork opportunities permitted.

> And fourth, the replies indicate that there are twenty-two
> institutions which seem reasonably likely to provide teaching,
> more teaching or fieldwork practice in community work, or in
> some way to strengthen the community work content of their

present courses. A respondent said: 'It is the view of the Department that if the social and personal problems which face many citizens are to be dealt with in more than a largely irrelevant manner it will be necessary to extend social work practice into the area of community work, especially in view of the need being so much greater than can be met by casework services'.

The developments above appear to be based on assumptions that community work, as a method of social work, is 'a good thing'; that it has come to stay; that it can be taught; and that it is based on recognisable or identifiable principles and practice. Respondents at seven institutions submitted memoranda or papers of some length setting out the case for community work teaching, including theory and fieldwork.

The considerable increase in the number of courses teaching about community work, with or without fieldwork, is, as we have said, the reverse of what the Study Group thought desirable for a 'strategy of training'. Perhaps inevitably in an uncontrolled situation with much pressure on institutions to introduce community work teaching, its plea for a few 'centres of excellence' in advance of general expansion has been ignored. The pressure for community work courses has come from staff and students themselves, from the larger number of community or quasi-community work appointments, particularly in social services or social work departments and education services, and from changing perceptions of the nature of social work. There has been a shift from concentration on casework to a new concept of social work, based on ability to assess a social situation and intervene in whatever seems to be the most effective way, whether primarily with the individual, family, group or community or with other social systems; this has led to the conclusion that even social workers who will practise primarily as caseworkers must have some abilities in and intelligent understanding of community work. Thus the trend to include community work in social work and youth work courses arises from the nature of changes in the situation since 1968. These trends are likely to continue.

As might be expected, the enquiry shows that there are many difficulties about fieldwork. In the nature of things, good placements and experienced field teachers did not exist but had to be created. Some courses only give some theoretical teaching in community work; others require visits of observation or a project. Others on the contrary think supervised fieldwork essential if students are to begin to gain some competence in practice. Staff, field teachers and students alike are finding it difficult to be clear about the nature and boundaries of community work 'in the live'. It is also proving very difficult to decide what students should be expected to achieve by the end of a field placement. Even if they have been able to get some small project started, they are not usually in the agency long enough to carry it through. On the other hand it is difficult to give them sufficiently clearly defined responsibilities in a continuing piece of community work. The struggle to give form and substance to community fieldwork placements and to link these with the theoretical studies is also reflected in a similar struggle to clarify what should go into supervisors' reports; though naturally the content of the fieldwork and the content of supervisors' reports are closely linked with each other, and lead on to further problems about how to evaluate students' progress.

Current issues in training for community work

Students need sufficiently long and well planned community fieldwork placements to enable them to assess the effectiveness of services at the point of delivery; to realise the constraints, complexities and demands of any work situation, including radical 'grass roots' activities; and to judge the most effective moment and method of intervention in the interests of the community groups they will serve. It is also essential that those who teach community work should remain in close contact with its practice; and that field teachers should meet regularly at the university or college from which they take students to clarify the most useful field experiences for students, including both systematic observation and responsibility for some segment of community work. The aim of fieldwork is of course to develop an acceptable level of skill and 'know-how' over a reasonable range of activities. All the foregoing terms imply judgment and measurement. But none of this is as yet at all clearly worked out. The task of relating theory and practice to each other (including relevant knowledge from the social sciences and political theory) should rest with field teachers as well as with classroom teachers. This again points to the need for close co-operation and also for clarity about the difference between the content of any given field experience and effective educational method. At its best the type of field teaching developed in casework has proved an exceptionally sound means of teaching professional practice. Much of the content of the task is different in community work and casework; but there may be much that is similar in educational method. Systematic and recorded study is desirable here. The third partner in discovering the nature of good community fieldwork is of course the student. If students learn most vividly through their own experience and if community work is about participation, then their experience and what they make of it at different stages is a key element in the whole process of teaching and learning through actual practice.

From a number of the returns to the enquiry about the current status of training for community work it seems as though many teachers of the subject are overburdened, with too little time for study, for regular meetings with each other, for close contact with practice and for the demanding activities entailed in 'creating' field teachers in community work. Yet advances in education for community work depend on this. Equally clearly, both teaching staffs and practitioners in community projects gain from regular seminar discussions, and thus an in-service training contribution is made to practice in the locality. Perhaps ideally this liaison between the two groups directed towards improving student supervision should be the main responsibility of one member of the teaching staff with adequate time for the purpose. Even a few appointments of this kind might demonstrate their value. The community work course at Glasgow University is an example of close links between the university and practice, since the full-time supervisor of a student unit teaches at the university for a day a week, while the community work teacher goes into field practice. There are also monthly meetings for community workers, attended by thirty to fifty people.

To a large extent community work teachers and supervisors too are working in isolation with little chance to discuss their teaching, their problems, their successes and their hunches with each other. Regular regional meetings, periodic seminars on specific subjects and above all the resource centres which we propose in chapter 8 would all strengthen and support pioneer efforts in training for community work. Moreover the resources of the CCETSW will become increasingly available and should be used to the full.

It is as true now as it was in 1968 (Gulbenkian Foundation, 1968, p. 150) that:

> Much effort will be needed to provide adequate community work teaching and fieldwork . . . Student units are desirable for fieldwork. It is also essential that . . . courses should have sufficient staff to supervise students, to give extra help to inexperienced field teachers, to collect and edit case records and other teaching material and to meet regularly for consultation about the content of the courses and student assessment.
> One year 'cadetships' or 'internships' near a course centre to enable newly qualified community workers to consolidate their skill under supervision would be an effective means of producing better qualified community workers, supervisors and teachers.

The nature of the community worker's task

Rather surprisingly, none of the respondents raised any serious queries, uncertainties or desire for more knowledge about the task or tasks for which community work students were being prepared. The Study Group's classification of community work into 'grass roots' or neighbourhood work, inter-agency activities and community planning (Gulbenkian Foundation, 1968, p. 35) seems to be generally accepted, but with little analysis of the range of competence required in practice or what light this throws on the content of training, whether in theoretical studies or fieldwork. We were constantly brought up short in discussions about training by this lack of 'hard' information about the knowledge, competence and attitudes demanded by different forms of community work. This makes it difficult to know whether, for example, particular attitudes towards people and certain natural gifts in individual and group relations are more fundamental than, or indeed a sufficient substitute for, knowledge; or whether the guidance of knowledge also becomes both essential and possible as more 'usable' knowledge becomes available.

In discussion at a full meeting of the Community Work Group led by practising community workers (already summarised in more detail in chapter 3, pp. 23–5), it was agreed that since they are practitioners in group situations they must have a knowledge of group dynamics, what is happening in a group, the interaction of individuals and the effect of different personalities, including how to cope with natural leaders who may dominate the group. The essential skills in human relationships include how to work effectively with different groups ranging from those with practically no social skills to others with a wide span of knowledge and social competence, how to maintain interest, how to make constructive use of conflict as well as agreement, how to communicate with indigenous groups on the one hand and with senior officials and members of other professions on the other hand. This would include giving practical information, collecting data and presenting it in statistical form, using adult education methods and communication skills, as well as systematically recording what is being done in order to evaluate methods and outcome. This brief account obviously telescopes wide areas of knowledge and assumes the high degree of self-awareness and integrity demanded in community work.

It may well be that the research being undertaken in the government-sponsored community development projects will cast more light on the whole subject. In any event, training should on no account be divorced from systematic study of community work practice and demands. In saying this we are well aware of the pitfalls of trying to assess 'success' or 'failure'. None the less this is a poor reason for not studying the nature of the tasks in community work in its different forms as these are evolving under the pressure of experience. *Community Work and Social Change* (p. 149) concluded that: 'a detailed study of practice would make an essential contribution to training' and (p. 151) that 'continuing research, recording and analysis of practice, and evaluation of the relation of training to the needs of the field are all essential, both to the improvement of training and practice and also in due time to make advanced training possible. In particular, research should be built into each stage of certain in-service and full-time training courses from the planning stage, through to students' subsequent performance in their first appointments.'

The need for better documentation of methods and techniques being used by community workers, of their outcome and of the demands of the job is even greater now than it was in 1968. There are by this time many more professionally trained community workers in employment, and evaluation of their training in relation to their subsequent work experience should also help to make training more directly relevant to the demands of community work. Continuous analysis of the nature of the task—or tasks—in community work is not wholly the responsibility of educational institutions. But neither is it at present anyone else's responsibility. There is a serious gap here which could lead to wasteful use of teaching resources, together with misdirected effort by newly qualified community workers and, in time, to disillusionment when reality proves stubbornly intransigent.

So far, most of the limelight in training for community work in this country seems to be focused on 'grass roots' or neighbourhood work and little on inter-agency co-ordination or community planning. In the United States the sheer magnitude of American social problems has pushed action in the direction of institutional change, rather than assuming that community work with a sufficient number of individuals or groups would bring about a change in social institutions. This has resulted in the use of confrontation and conflict, of advocacy and community action. Professor Nathan Cohen in a review of *Community Work and Social Change* in *International Social Work* (1971, pp. 58–9) is critical because 'The concepts of power, confrontation, conflict and advocacy seem singularly absent. There also seems to be greater emphasis on administrative and inter-organisational planning than on social problems and social policy planning.' He also questions the emphasis on inter-personal relations, since agents of institutional change also require knowledge of political science, socio-political and economic theory. The shift in attitudes in this country since 1968, particularly towards the use of conflict, advocacy, community action and social reform, have narrowed the gap between these two approaches, although there is comparatively little emphasis on bringing about structural change from within the system rather than through confrontation and conflict.

The lack of training for social planning

In evidence to the sub-group, a chief planning officer and a partner in a large firm of architects both deplored the lack of any professional practitioners competent to assess the social problems and the present and probable future needs of an area and to work in an inter-disciplinary team with physical planners. This demands people trained to assess and understand the social structure and needs of a particular community and to predict the best forms of social develop-ment for the future. At present, the results of consultation with local people about their community needs tend to be presented in a piecemeal, amateur fashion by community workers. Social scientists, on the other hand, are primarily observers and analysts, not practi-tioners in partnership with physical planners; they are therefore reluctant, so it was said, to commit themselves to decisions about planning based upon their observations. None the less, sociologists have played a part in the planning of new or extended towns.

No existing training course appears to meet this need for practi-tioners in community planning. There has indeed been relatively little progress in differentiating a specialist role of community planner, either at local authority or central government level, from the existing roles of physical planner or 'generalist' administrator; and therefore little progress has been made in training in this field. Nevertheless, the growth of planning divisions in relevant central government departments like the Department of the Environment and the Depart-ment of Health and Social Security, and the development of research branches of social services or social work departments of local authorities, are likely to increase the demand for greater specialist expertise in the field of community planning.

The findings of an American study on the community organisation curriculum in graduate schools of social work are relevant in this context. The study, which was undertaken by Dr Arnold Gurin for the United States Council on Social Work Education (1970), contains a detailed survey of the content and teaching methods being used in a number of university graduate schools of social work, though of course professional training for social planning in the USA is not confined to such schools. The study was primarily concerned with community organisation and social planning. Its recommendations are divided into two major categories:

a. *Foundation courses* to give students background knowledge, with the main emphasis on:

1   social behaviour based on material drawn from psychology, anthropology and micro-sociology, with focus on the behaviour of people in relation to social systems and including such subjects as role theory, group dynamics, small group behaviour, communication and decision-making;

2   institutional analysis, including relevant social sciences knowledge about institutions drawn from macro-sociology,

economics and political science with especial reference to
the sociology of the community, organisational theory,
social stratification, power structures, urban economics
and politics. Social policy and social welfare, including
major contemporary policy issues, methods of policy
analysis and evaluation are regarded as crucial subjects.

b. *Practice courses* concerned with the content of the tasks
performed by the practitioner, with the purpose of integrating
knowledge, methodology and skill. Three core practice courses
are proposed:

1 an introduction to the full range of practice in community
   organisation and social planning;
2 a course in methods of organisation; and
3 a course in methods of planning.

The study emphasises that social science research is an essential
tool for community organisers and social planners, who should thus
take courses in research to give them understanding of the values and
uses of research as an instrument in problem identification, a device
for obtaining needed information, a convenient entrée to the community and a way of influencing power centres. This teaching would
include the design of research for different purposes, methods of
collecting and analysing data and problems of measurement. The
study includes a detailed discussion of the content of both the core
and practice courses, which is of considerable value from the point
of view of developments in training for community work in this
country. Recently one or two university or other courses in social
planning have been introduced here. More courses are projected in
university departments of sociology or social administration. It
would be regrettable if these courses were divorced from training for
community work, more particularly if the 'community perspective'
were lacking in them and if two groups of students emerged with
unrelated qualifications and career prospects.

Should community work be a professional activity? Conflicting attitudes

Underlying community work, and therefore training for it, are several
opposed attitudes. There are those who see work with communities
as a form of social work intervention, allied to social work with
individuals, families, groups and in residential situations; they would
deplore its emergence as a separate specialisation. Others with equal
strength of conviction see it as a separate professional activity,
related to but distinct from both social work and education, which
must be helped as quickly as possible to stand on its own feet. To
others it is clearly a part of adult education with little or no relation

to social work. To yet others it is an element in a modern concept of administration, rather than having any particular affinity with either education or social work. On another view community work is basically a political activity aimed at change which will inevitably cause dissension; therefore community workers should have a sophisticated training in political theory and social action and may have to work outside a bureaucratic system. Others still would recognise the 'community perspective' in various professional activities—including work in the mass media—but regard real community work as something essentially spontaneous, local and incapable of becoming in any sense professional without losing its essence.

Some would maintain that to make community work professional would tend to increase the distance between the worker and the community, while in any event some of those most successful in neighbourhood work come from a variety of backgrounds. At present there is an 'open market' in community work, whereas training would restrict its development and diversification. All that is implied in the term 'community work' is so major a social development that we should explore its ramifications further, recognise that our present performance is inadequate and keep the boundaries fluid, rather than laying down rules that would inevitably be restrictive.

Those in favour of development in a professional direction argue that there is already a large and growing body of people engaged full time in community work who need the support which a clear identity, training, a code of the ethics of practice, research and a strong professional association would give them, as well as providing better protection for the public. Moreover, both training and practice would gain from a two-way flow of knowledge and experience, while community workers would be trained in a method applicable in a wide variety of situations, rather than operating without common professional standards and mainly concentrating upon specific settings. Such a development would mean the identification of a body of knowledge and practice skills belonging primarily to community work, with related professional standards and code of ethics.

It is precisely here that conflict centres because what some see as the urgent task of identifying the concepts which underlie the processes and practice of community work is to others a deplorable attempt to straitjacket a fluid, changing activity, for which in any event there is no solid body of knowledge at present on which to base training. It is small wonder if in such a divisive situation there is no common policy about training for community work, no agreement as to whether it is primarily social work, youth work, adult education or none of these, and no control over the mushroom growth of courses and qualifications. Indeed the only effective machinery for exercising such control is the CCETSW, whose writ obviously runs only within its own field. That Council is expected, within the context of social work, to promote and recognise training in community work. It has set up a curriculum study group to consider the objectives and content of syllabi in community work and it is likely that this group will produce a discussion document on the subject. In any event, as has been said above, many existing social work courses already include a good deal of teaching and field experience in 'grass roots' community work and some elements of community organisation and planning.

The controversy as to whether community work is primarily social work, adult education, or a mixture of both, or neither, naturally turns on definitions and the characteristics of practice. It is now accepted in social work that it is, as in the early days of the settlement movement, concerned with the local community as well as with individuals and small groups. For example, the recent stress on community care rather than care in institutions has inevitably forced social workers to try to develop greater skill in mobilising community resources, acceptance and support for the old, the handicapped, immigrants, ex-psychiatric patients, ex-prisoners and others. In addition, it is manifestly absurd to try to lessen individual stress if the cause lies mainly in community deficiencies, whether negative attitudes or lack of play-space or bad housing or poverty or whatever it may be. Hence the social work departments in Scotland and social services departments in England and Wales are committed to community work on all three levels of the classification in *Community Work and Social Change* (p. 35). This means that inevitably more community work will become part of the qualifying courses in social work, since these departments are far the largest employers of social workers.

Advanced training in social work is only developing slowly but such courses, whether primarily in management studies, community work or social planning and policy, are certain to expand in the coming decade. This also enhances current views of social work as essentially concerned with guided social change, with making it more possible for individuals, groups or communities to exercise responsible choice and with helping to forecast the likely consequences of specific change (for instance, population movements) and acting as a shock-absorber of change. Where the social worker's responsibility lies if the main resistance to change comes not from the clients but from those in authority is an increasingly debated question which students should confront in their training.

Many people in adult education regard social work as concerned only with deviance and pathology or with manipulating the non-conformers to adapt to the *status quo*, rather than having any part to play in improving the quality of life for normal people. On this view, community work is very much nearer to adult education than to social work, since both have the same objective of greater independence for the group and the growth of rationality and each uses some of the same methods. None the less, although adult education is highly relevant to community work it is not synonymous with it. Community development may be adult education in its broadest sense, since its objectives are to help people to identify their social problems and consider what action to take. But community organisation (inter-agency and community planning) is not necessarily related to adult education. Conversely, it is not the aim of all adult education to identify social needs in order to bring about change. For example, the primary purpose of a course on exotic fish would be to increase the students' knowledge rather than to promote social interaction.

Adult education commonly refers to groups sponsored by local education authorities, university extra-mural departments or the Workers' Educational Association, with a tutor or teacher in the class, directed towards increasing knowledge and developing skills, sensitivity and creativity by means of intellectual, cultural and recreative pursuits, generally in a non-vocational and voluntary context. The term is used more loosely to include, for instance, educational broadcasting and activity in community centres. So far, adult education has largely failed to reach the less privileged social groups. Some wish therefore to develop it on less academic lines and in a form less subject- and classroom-based. The stimulation and leadership of socially and politically oriented action is in fact providing, notably through community development projects, a new kind of adult education which shares at one end an indeterminate boundary with community work. A significant example of adult education in a working-class community, linking community schools, residents' groups and community councils will be found in the Halsey report (1972, pp. 159–60).

At the opposite end of the spectrum from the foregoing is the view that adult education should have nothing directly to do with, and in some cases must indirectly run counter to, predetermined aspirations of the teachers concerned, for political, social or community changes.

It is clear to us that some of the skills used by community workers come from adult education and some from social work, while others are specific to neither but used by both. It would be a mistake to try to fix frontiers, which will continue to shift. But continuous co-operation between adult education and community work practitioners, teachers and organisations is vital. Each needs to know what others are doing and to explore avenues of mutual help. Their use at times of the same knowledge and skills suggests the value of some training in common for their workers; and community work is already found in the syllabus of study in a number of adult classes (see also 'In-service training', p. 123 below). We hope that various aspects of this whole issue will be clarified when the reports of the Russell Committee,* set up in 1969 for England and Wales, and the Alexander Committee† set up in 1970 for Scotland, are available.

As a result of our examination of social work, teacher and youth and community work training in both graduate and undergraduate courses, we found ourselves speculating about a possible reorganisation of the objectives and patterns of training so as to provide more integrated and purposeful programmes of study which relate to subsequent careers. Our speculations have led us to the conclusion that the existing patterns of training and careers in teaching, social work and youth and community work need to be reviewed, especially the routes for entry to training courses and for proceeding from training into practice; the object would be to avoid *culs-de-sac*. The appropriate bodies should also consider how people trained in other professions can best be re-oriented by means of 'conversion' courses, if they wish to transfer to careers predominantly in the community work field. The report of the James Committee (1971), the Halsey report (1972), the recent establishment of the CCETSW and the general climate of change in patterns of higher education provide opportunities which should not be lost. We hope that existing inter-professional frontiers, both for practice and for training, will not obstruct such a review.

The community element in certain other occupations

We carried this question further than the original Study Group report by having discussions with or seeking information or illustrative material from people in the fields of planning, architecture, general practice, education, administration, the churches, the law and in relation to police training. The results were necessarily impressionistic but they showed that there has been a quite dramatic increase in recent years in perception of the direct relevance to various professional practices of articulate understanding of community processes, of responsibility to identify and take action about specific community ills, and of the need to consult people about decisions which affect their lives. This includes professional responsibility to keep systematic records of individual cases for the analysis of social needs, to use

* Terms of reference: 'To assess the need for and to review the provision of non-vocational adult education in England and Wales; to consider the appropriateness of existing educational, administrative and financial policies; and to make recommendations with a view to obtaining the most effective and economical deployment of available resources to enable adult education to make its proper contribution to the national system of education conceived of as a process continuing through life.' The report was published in March 1973.

† Terms of reference: 'To consider the aims appropriate to voluntary leisure-time courses for adults which are educational but not specifically vocational; to examine the extent to which these are being achieved at present; and, with due regard to the need to use available resources most effectively, to make recommendations.'

these records to identify trends and high risk groups, and to take inter-disciplinary and co-operative action where community needs are unmet, and also as an aid to focusing community work as such. Obvious examples are the stress created by urban renewal plans or by actual rehousing or the changed attitudes required to use family planning facilities, or to accept newcomers to the area. In general this responsibility means being sufficiently free from professional and bureaucratic constraints to be constantly concerned about what happens to people for whom services are provided.

More specifically, so far as *planners* and *architects* are concerned, training is clearly of great importance from the community point of view and our enquiries showed that this is beginning to be recognised. There is no specific reference to communities or community work in the Royal Institute of British Architects' (RIBA) own examination syllabus, though for the final examination the student should have some acquaintance with 'what is being talked about and written in the areas of social studies relating the built environment to man and his place in society'. The major educational effort in architecture is now conducted in Schools of Architecture recognised by the RIBA. 'Syllabuses, orientation, direction and end product vary widely amongst these schools' as 'the RIBA does not lay down guide syllabuses but positively encourages variety and experiment' (communication from the RIBA). Within the schools of architecture there is increasing interest in community projects and in improving the quality of life of communities. The impetus for this comes, we are informed, 'co-incidentally from students, staff and institutional education bodies'. Particularly in the fourth and fifth years, when they are often encouraged to choose their own design topics, many students involve themselves in community studies or community projects.

The new planning syllabus for the final examination of the Royal Town Planning Institute (RTPI), which came into operation in 1970, is specific about the community aspects of studies. A three-hour examination is set to test the candidate's knowledge of 'the social and economic factors influencing the physical environment and his understanding of the relationship between planning and the social and economic disciplines'. The social factors are concerned with 'social structure, community concepts, and the relationships between planning and the planned'. These include 'community and neighbourhood concepts and studies; influence on planning theory and physical development; attitudes to home and environment; and consideration of social needs in the planning of urban and rural settlement' (RTPI, 1971).

The amount of emphasis on and formal teaching about community work varies in different planning courses. A lecturer in sociology in the Department of Town and Country Planning in one university writes: 'social planning and community development studies are dealt with at a rather general level at present but I would like to see them developed'. The head of the department in another university says: 'we feel that training for planning should include not only knowledge but practical experience in the attitudes and priorities of local communities and their particular interests'. He goes on to say: 'we have found in practice that the most serious difficulty preventing satisfactory teaching in this particular area has been the lack of any suitably qualified and experienced persons', and adds that they have failed to recruit a lecturer in social studies related to planning.

The enquiries of the sub-group in this field have necessarily been limited but we think it important that the implications for community work training of current trends in education for architecture and planning should be studied in detail. This is particularly urgent in relation to planning at the present time when the RTPI has been re-examining its own role and education policy in relation to the existing profession and to social and economic planning. This is also obviously related to what we say earlier about training for social planning.

In the training of *medical students* who intend to become general practitioners, the trend towards emphasising the community setting has been much encouraged by the recent foundation of departments of general practice in a series of universities. The student is, increasingly, introduced to the behavioural sciences, including sociology and social anthropology; and taught to understand the interdependence of the preventive and social services in the community and its expression through teamwork in general practice and through health centres. More stress has come to be laid also on community psychiatry, as well as on the nature of the doctor-patient relationship in the community setting. Registered medical practitioners who intend to become members of the Royal College of General Practitioners must complete a recognised three-year training in general practice and pass examinations which include human development; human behaviour; and 'society and medicine'. Relevant as background to these developments is Appendix 11 of the Todd Commission report of 1968, which sets out a specimen syllabus in social factors related to medicine.

The syllabus for the training of *health visitors* includes the development of the individual and the pressures that may be exerted on him by the society in which he lives, including attitudes towards handicapped or deviant people. This sets health visitors' work within a community context (CETHV, 1970, p. 52):

As the health visitor is concerned with the promotion and maintenance of good health, it is essential that she should be able to identify those features of the environment which make for ill health; she can then consider to what extent she contributes to minimising their influence. Her work provides the opportunity of seeing where community resources fall short or where the individual people with whom she is in touch are unable to use them. As a fieldworker she is in a good position to inform [those] who are responsible for community services about detrimental factors in environment and services.

The Briggs Committee (1972) proposes a unification of training for both hospital and community nurses.

So far as the training of *teachers* is concerned, institutes of education, university education departments and colleges of education are trying to varying extents and in different ways to give students an effective insight into the complexities of local community life, with the school as one amongst other institutions concerned with improvements in the quality of life. Lecture courses on the social services or the child and the family are of course not community work though they may be a useful background. 'Often it is hard to know what is happening because so many strangers gather under the umbrella marked "community studies"' (Milson, 1972). In a few courses there are substantial options called by various titles but entailing an understanding of community processes and including fieldwork. Some students during their teaching practice in EPA schools or elsewhere are given real opportunities to take part in community work, whether school-based or otherwise. It is recognised now to an increasing extent that students need to see how people, statutory services and voluntary bodies interact in a variety of communities in response to different issues. Their studies should arise from contemporary problems and include opportunities for first-hand observation.

Experiments with dual role posts like counselling, careers advisers or home-school liaison teachers also result in more teaching with a social content in teacher training. As an example of new trends, Ilkley College of Education has started in the current (1972) session a three-year course in community education which is designed to give teachers experience of community needs and problems.

The curriculum for the training of teachers will have to undergo a sea change in directions already discernible if the concept of community schools spreads widely and if such schools are to discover how 'to equip the rising generation with the knowledge and skills to cope with, give power over and in the end to transform the conditions of their local community' (Halsey, 1972, p. 12).

All young *administrators* in central government whether from social or other departments, are now required to take training at the Civil Service College, part of which is designed to increase their social awareness. Advanced training is also available at more senior levels. An increasing number of key people in local government, such as directors of housing and directors of social services, are taking courses at the Institute of Local Government Studies in the University of Birmingham or elsewhere, with the support of the Local Government Training Board. Courses for assistant directors and area officers are provided at several educational institutions. Those at the National Institute for Social Work Training devote a day to community work and community participation; the latter includes a session with members of a tenants' association.

There is clear evidence that in the training of *ministers and clergy* the community work aspect of their professional role is taken more and more seriously. This emphasis is at present the concern mainly of a relatively few enthusiastic pioneers among the ordained, who have tried to practise community work in churches of various denominations or other religious organisations. Courses of training for clergy include a growing community work content, either as part of a basic theological training, as at Queen's College, Birmingham, or as in-service or secondary training.

Significant changes have also been taking place in the *legal profession*. The growth of interest in social legislation, the development of experimental legal advice centres and the interest among many young lawyers in helping consumers of the public services to obtain their rights are all leading to the recognition of the need for a greater emphasis in legal education on studies in social policy and the social sciences. The Nuffield Foundation is sponsoring several projects aimed at establishing links between lawyers and social scientists.

So far as *the police* are concerned, the report of the Working Party on Police Training in Race Relations, 1971, shows the direction of current thought (pp. 2, 6, 7):

> The police service must respond to changes in society and must possess some understanding of the different groups that make up the community . . . and . . . place all race relations training within the wider context of the relations between the police and the community at large. It could equally well be referred to as training in community relations . . . [It] should deal in broad terms with the economic and social difficulties of urban areas, and the special problems of communication . . . between . . . representatives of authority . . . and members of the poorer and less articulate classes. [The argument is then that] training should give the police officer (from cadets to senior officers) an understanding of . . . (a) psychological mechanisms such as 'scapegoating' and 'stereotyping' . . . (c) the effects of prejudice and discrimination upon minorities.

The report* also approves of cadets taking part in community service projects on an equality with other young people and advocates such methods of changing attitudes as small mixed discussion

* A limited number of copies are available from the Home Office.

groups and role play. These enlightened attitudes in police training are much to be welcomed.

Communities, work places and residential institutions

Some of us think that the term 'community' cannot be restricted to geographical areas. Some functional groups, for instance those bound by strong religious or racial ties, seem to have a number of similar characteristics: as indeed do such institutions as factories or other commercial enterprises, hospitals, schools, prisons, colleges and universities. Further light is being cast on these functional inter-group relations by various studies of the sociology of institutions as social systems and of staff-resident relations within them. So far as we know, limited use is at present made of these studies as an element in the training of those who work in such situations. None the less an increasing number of students of sociology, social administration and social work study the sociology of institutions, both theoretically and through participant observation. Moreover, personnel managers in training, for example, study industrial sociology, including group and inter-group relations and attitudes, as well as characteristics of the outside community, especially as these impinge upon the work situation.

The general relevance of community studies

In our view, the initial study of community structure, relations and changing patterns is an element in the education of citizens which should not be delayed until the professional training stage nor confined within certain professional trainings. Rather, it might well be taught at appropriate levels during the school years, using material from economics, sociology, psychology, demography, geography and history, so as to help boys and girls to develop an intelligent understanding of the changing society in which they live. This study would be reinforced by voluntary social service activities and direct observation if these are properly related to main studies. It would lay the foundation for more specific study and practice later by some young people in a variety of professional trainings. What we have in mind for all schools is eloquently expressed for EPA schools in the Halsey report (p. 195):

> EPA community education, as an element in community development, is about moving on, not standing still. It is about the formation of social personalities with the attributes of constructive discontent. It is about children who are made eager apprentices of community life. It presumes that an educational priority area should be radically reformed and that its children, as junior citizens, should be forewarned and forearmed for the struggle.

Teachers need to be sensitive to the social and moral climate in which their children are growing up. The application of teaching virtues to a compassionate, tolerant and critical examination of all social, political and moral issues is the highest hurdle along the road to a community-oriented curriculum. It could take years and it will require a generous and sympathetic change of heart, not only among educational authorities but in society at large.

We agree with those who say that basic training in the under-standing of human behaviour and of social structure and relationships should be undertaken in common for a variety of professions, thus laying the foundation for an interdisciplinary, 'in the round' approach to human functioning in various social situations. The illustrations from different professions earlier in this chapter show that study of community relationships, use of this knowledge and acceptance of people's right to express their views and take part in decision-making processes becomes more directly necessary, indeed an essential element, in different professional tasks, as members of a given profession take on wider responsibilities on promotion. It should be recognised that a danger common to all those intervening within the community is that of projecting their own views and perceptions into any situation; training should help them to rip off their pro-fessional blinkers and to become more aware of and sensitive to the social and psychological forces within individuals (including them-selves) and within and between groups. It goes without saying that such teaching should be given by those who are competent in the subject.

In-service training

The original Study Group thought that extensive in-service training would do even more to raise standards and provide support for community workers than limited expansion of full-time courses. This is all the more pressing now since community workers and community work projects are both increasing. In-service training is, amongst other things, a means of promoting inter-agency community planning and action and of bringing into structured discussion the continuing experience of field workers and their contribution to common knowledge and standards. This is especially effective when in-service courses are so planned as to build on the different experience and perspectives of participants.

It has not been possible to get comprehensive information about what is happening at present in a diffuse field with ill-defined boundaries, whether of function or content of courses. It is therefore only possible to give illustrations. The National Council of Social Service has initiated a series of inter-disciplinary part-time courses in different parts of the country over the last few years, for staff of both voluntary and statutory agencies engaged in community work and of other professions specially concerned with the community. The five courses in 1972 were held at Brunel, Exeter, Leicester, Liverpool and York Universities.

A number of community councils or councils of social service run courses for volunteers or members of professions active in community work, some in co-operation with university adult education, external or extension departments. These departments and also polytechnics, colleges of education and further education and other educational institutions are taking a greater initiative than in 1968 to provide courses either on or related to community work. For example, the Liverpool University Institute of Extension Studies calculates that between 1968 and 1972 about 1,000 students have participated in courses and conferences with a considerable community work content. The aim is to stimulate people, whether voluntary workers or professionals, to study practical community problems. The usual teaching media are seminars and conferences in which members contribute from their own experience.

The Young Volunteer Force Foundation and other organisations provide training weekends for their staff. The in-service training of local authority youth and community workers has recently included to a limited extent the theory and practice of community work. In other respects, a sample enquiry suggests that local authorities, which are the largest employers in this field, provide very little in-service training in community work at present; but there are signs that some social services or social work departments in particular are concerned at the lack of systematic training for community work and are ready for action.

Progress since 1968 has been uneven, despite marked initiative in some quarters. This is a serious gap in provision since those in this field need constantly to bring their experience up to date and to dispute controversial issues with colleagues who have different work experiences or backgrounds. A co-ordinated assault on this largely unoccupied territory is called for: we suggest that the CCETSW should meet with representatives of university extra-mural and adult education departments, colleges of education and others in the education field and with the principal statutory and voluntary employers, with community workers and others, to ventilate the subject and consider the best means of devising a continuous and co-ordinated programme of in-service training for community work; an integrated programme is required for all staff concerned with the community (not only for those called community workers) in both voluntary and statutory services. The programme should be related to varying types of experience and should make the most economical use of scarce training resources.

Training for members of self-help groups and volunteers

Problems of definition are even more difficult here than for salaried people who are wholly or partly engaged in community work. Active members of a tenants' association or a claimants' union are clearly community workers. Volunteer playgroup leaders may or may not be. What about members of Alcoholics Anonymous or the Samaritans? In short, when does any form of voluntary social service in the community become community work? No clear answer can be given to these questions. Moreover community groups consisting of or including volunteers do not by any means agree on the value of training. Some would maintain that it is wholly unnecessary, while others would aim only to bring staff and volunteers together occasionally for a general discussion of their work and its progress or difficulties. Some organisations such as the Child Poverty Action Group run a number of courses on citizens' welfare rights which have attracted a cross-section of the community. In addition, a good many university extra-mural departments, polytechnics, technical colleges and institutes offer lectures and discussions on topical community issues or information courses on the law, citizens' rights and so on. It would not be realistic to expect or propose a systematic training programme here. But we wish to urge on community organisations which encourage volunteers that they should at least ensure that these have a thorough induction, either by working alongside an experienced employee or through a regular course, before they enter the field actively themselves.

Regular help and support to local community groups to enable them to study and define their problems, to discover their rights and learn how to take collective action is in a broad sense in-service training. It is carried on in many different ways whether by individuals or through community development projects or other organisations, including EPA community schools. There is a particularly interesting example in Liverpool where the WEA tutor-organiser is a member of the Education Priority Area team, with adult education accepted as an essential part of the community school. This has included establishing links with residents, groups and community councils, encouraging discussion, helping local groups to learn through doing and, through a variety of activities, to contribute to the process of community development and change.

Conclusions

The following conclusions may be drawn about desirable developments over the next few years from our discussions about current trends.

This review of the present situation shows that much more training for community work is included in social work courses now than in 1968 and that this trend is gathering momentum, while youth and community work courses and a few courses in community work as such have come into existence. Some who teach these subjects to students who intend to become community workers use such material as is available to them; others deny that this is yet a subject capable of substantial teaching or of professional practice. Practice itself is also in an embryonic stage, especially so far as students' fieldwork is concerned, with confusion about how to give focus and direction to their activities, how supervisors themselves should be trained, what they should teach and how students' progress should be evaluated. There is a real danger of divorce between teaching and practice, both because systematically recorded and evaluated field studies are lacking and because community work teachers have too little time for close contact with projects, and neither time nor opportunity to exchange views amongst themselves. We think there should be urgent consultations amongst all the interests concerned to work out means of remedying these deficiencies, which could lead to a widening gap between theory and practice.

One part of a strategy of training would be continuing study groups on curriculum content and planning, on fieldwork and on in-service training. It would also be desirable to have parallel study groups on the ethics of community intervention and on the application of the social sciences in training and in practice. It goes without saying that these study groups should be closely related to developments in the practice of community work in its various forms. The proposed CCETSW study groups will help to meet these needs, especially if they include both community work teachers and practitioners and also members from the field of adult education and social scientists familiar with community studies. Changing ideas about the range of community work would also make it desirable to include the contribution of subjects like political theory and organisation theory.

We think the earlier Study Group was right in suggesting a limited number of well-staffed community work courses which would make the best use of and add to limited resources. Even though actual developments have been different over the past few years, we think there is a strong case for a few courses to become 'centres of excellence' which might provide resources for consultation, study and the exchange of information, as well as setting standards in student training.

In present training the limelight falls on direct neighbourhood work but there is also a need for systematic training at the interagency and planning levels of community work. Community development, community organisation and community or social planning all include elements of each other and it would be unfortunate if there were to be a concentration on direct neighbourhood work or on social planning in courses unrelated to each other. This is a matter for consideration by the JUC.

We were constantly faced by the lack of 'hard' information about the range of knowledge and competence needed in different kinds of community work, the extent to which particular personal qualities are necessary for success and what light students' subsequent experience in employment casts on the necessary content of training. At present there is no clear responsibility for making such studies.

There is also an unfortunate separation between courses which come under the social work umbrella and those in youth and community work which come under the area training organisations (in Scotland the Consultative Council on Youth and Community Service). We hope that the whole situation will shortly be reviewed in the light of the James report and other considerations. We say this bearing in mind that a higher proportion of community workers to total staffs will be employed in social work services than in the much larger education services but also that community studies are likely to be increasingly significant as community schools and informal adult education both become more widespread. As we have said above, we think some adult education methods are necessary ingredients of community work.

The practice of community work is already becoming professionalised. The aim should be to incorporate relevant knowledge into both theoretical studies and field work in order to prepare students for the range of practice discussed in earlier chapters. This includes both their personal development and the professional integrity necessary to support community workers in difficult and sometimes lonely situations in which they must often face apathy, hostility and conflicting demands. All those concerned with the education of students for this new and changing practice face the dilemma of being clear about the objectives of community work and at the same time keeping the options open. In any event, it is desirable that standards should be regarded as more important than professionalism.

Increased action research and monitored experiments are necessary to clarify the nature of community work in different circumstances and to provide teaching material on its theory and practice. The need for such research, for edited case studies based upon the use of a framework such as we suggest in chapter 5 and for a service of abstracts of articles and other publications has already been mentioned in that chapter. Our own analysis of the material available to us and our discussions with various people in this field strongly reinforce the case for a national resource centre. It is obvious that such a centre would be valuable to community work as such and that it would greatly add to the supply and quality of teaching materials. It would also act as a forum for joint discussion, for seminars and conferences as well as for individual study. We hope that trusts as well as public authorities will be actively interested in the possibilities of this proposal, which is discussed fully in chapter 8.

The drive to include social studies—human relations in their individual and social contexts—in training for various professions in the public services has gained momentum. The need for this and for a community focus in various professions is obvious; the means are less clear. For some years past there have been discussions about the importance of inter-disciplinary training in human relations at the student stage. This is indeed important; but it becomes even more so at senior professional levels when the consequences for local community well-being, and thus the need for a well-informed approach to this, become very much greater because of the community aspects inherent in senior appointments. It may be that a fruitful starting point would be inter-disciplinary discussions among practising members of different professions about the contribution of each profession in relation to the others and about new dimensions of common or specific understanding of community to which each is trying to give greater precision. A related though different approach would be a closer coming together of 'public interventionists' or 'change agents', an inter-professional approach to promote a community orientation through discussion of specific community situations. The aim would be to break through departmental and professional rigidities. In any event, we think the time is ripe for a series of consultations with senior members of relevant professions about inter-disciplinary training in community studies.

8 Some present needs and proposals for meeting them

An assessment of present needs for the development of community work, with proposals for meeting these, was made by the working party referred to in chapter 1. The summary which follows includes the views of the Community Work Group as a whole, expressed at its final meeting in January 1973.

Needs and the ways of meeting them may be considered from two separate viewpoints:

the organisational and co-operative needs of community work itself;

the specific needs of different groups of people engaged or interested in community work, i.e.:
community groups,
community workers or organisations involved in community work, teachers of community work, and
those with a concern for the development of the various forms of community work: an inter-professional, inter-agency group.

The main needs of community work

Although there is considerable overlap between the various needs, they may be grouped under the following five headings:

Information

Local community groups and community workers need information on practical matters, for example on points to be considered when setting up a project, as well as continuous information about current developments and legislation. Information of this type is available but it has to be searched out and it is often not in a form useful to groups. It is obviously a waste of time for community workers to collate and interpret individually information for which there is a general demand; thus there is a need for a central agency to process and disseminate this material. But much of the information required by community groups is local to the neighbourhood, area or local

129

authority and does not lend itself to being collected or distributed nationally.

Teachers of community work need teaching materials, including analyses of projects, case studies, an abstracting service, a periodic newsletter, audio-visual aids and an annotated catalogue of community work literature.

Information services may be local or national. National services are required to ensure that the whole field is covered, that local experience is fully exchanged and shared and that information of value to all is expertly and economically collated and distributed. National services might in time assist in promoting local services. Information needs, particularly those of local groups, change quickly and it is essential that any central information agency should be flexible in meeting its clients' requirements.

A survey of information needs and services, specially commissioned by the Community Work Group, indicates that although much of the information required is in fact available from existing services, people are not necessarily aware of the services which do exist; the information is not available from any one place; and some information does not appear to have been systematically collected or made available. Any new service would have to resolve this present confused situation.

Advisory and supporting services

The problems of finding information 'at the grass roots' are closely linked with those of advice. Local groups frequently need advisory and supporting services as well as information. Advice could range from how to run committees to ways of obtaining the resources and equipment that groups need. The experience of organisations such as the Young Volunteer Force suggests that advice could best be provided by consultants or field officers. There may well be a case for a peripatetic group of experienced people who could provide training on the spot for members of groups. Such people should be based locally rather than centrally and in existing organisations rather than in new ones. Community groups are often in special need of technical aid from specialists in the use of equipment such as duplicators, printing machines, tape recorders, video tapes and display material. These should be made available at local area centres accessible to local groups. The centres should also keep records of local bodies willing to lend equipment to community groups.

Training

It is not only the academics and the administrators on the one hand and the practitioners on the other who have widely differing needs;

the same is true at local level as between the professional worker and the volunteer. Local groups might not take well to the idea of formal training and would react better to visits from an adviser and other kinds of informal training. There should for example be plenty of opportunities for exchanging views with other community groups and with those engaged in community work. Now that the Association of Community Workers (ACW) has moved (see p. 7), to a position where it becomes an association for community workers whether professionally qualified or not, members of local community groups would have the opportunity of sharing experiences and learning from professional colleagues in the process. Conversely, the professional workers would learn from the experience and feelings of members of groups. There is also a local need for people to learn how to tackle practical tasks such as running a community newspaper or a television or radio programme.

Professional community workers would always need in-service training courses and membership of a body like ACW might well be helpful. In addition, they and the teachers of community work would need information about training and careers, analyses of training and fieldwork and opportunities for meeting members of other professions with relevant interests. As has been said earlier, an element of information and concern for community work should form part of the training for other professions.

Although it would not be desirable to centralise full-time training for community work, it would be useful if there existed a central agency concerned to encourage suitable institutions to provide more training courses, including in-service training and training for members of local community groups not qualified for admission to existing courses. It would be particularly useful if there were a central agency able to give guidance about the content and emphases of existing community work courses, to supplement information already provided by such bodies as the Social Work Advisory Service. Community work training courses of all kinds undoubtedly need more publicity.

Funding

There are three distinct financial needs: resources for central purposes, resources for local supporting services and resources for local operational activities.

The amount and source of funds for central purposes would depend to some extent on the decision whether to set up a new agency, to attach a special new unit to an existing national organisation or to develop the functions of existing organisations. Certainly money would be needed for staff, administration, accommodation, information and advisory services, conferences, courses, studies and research.

Local supporting services would no doubt have to be financed largely from local statutory and voluntary funds but money should be sought to set up one or two local experiments, preferably outside London, in order to demonstrate the value of local centres and to encourage local, if not national, support for initiatives all over Britain.

There should be additional means of funding local community work projects. Sources might include government and foundations. Initial pump-priming and emergency support grants need to be made available quickly and with the minimum of red tape. Ideally, the fund should be administered by an independent body.

There is urgent need for all these types of funds and their establishment should be given high priority.

Forum function

There is much evidence to suggest that various interested groups of people would benefit from increased opportunities for getting together to exchange views and experiences. More explicitly, there seem to be various needs both nationally and locally for links and discussions—

between those approaching community work from different angles including adult education, youth and community work, social work and community action;

between those engaged in different aspects of community work including fieldwork, training and administration (this would help, for example, in relating the curriculum to community work practice);

between those in relevant organisations and professions (including planners, teachers, social workers, etc.);

between those in community groups and in the professions ('the planners and the planned');

between members of different community groups.

In addition, conferences, seminars and study groups to discuss particular issues are needed nationally, regionally and locally. Some of these needs have been met from time to time but more should be done in a co-ordinated way. No one is at present responsible for finding out what is going on, for spotting the gaps and for doing something to fill them, either by arranging conferences, etc. or by encouraging suitable bodies to provide them.

An independent forum open to all those interested, rather than a learned society, is needed to extend the valuable opportunities provided by the Gulbenkian Foundation, through the Community Work Group, for the wide discussion of community work. There is also a need for continuing discussion within an invited group of those concerned with policy or influential in official or academic circles.

What is or can be done by existing organisations

To discover the extent to which existing organisations are meeting or are interested to meet the identified needs, discussions were held with leading figures or groups of representatives from a number of key organisations, or information was gathered from these by correspondence. The following general conclusions were drawn from the valuable information obtained:

No existing organisation covers all or indeed a major part of any of the needs identified, but several are already deeply involved in some aspect or other of most of these needs and it would be an advantage for this to continue.

There is a great deal of information available in a number of existing organisations, but only to those who have the time and patience to find it.

A number of the organisations favour a small national resource centre or clearing house to be responsible for monitoring and promoting initiatives in the development of community work.

There does not seem to be any conflict between the responsibilities of the organisations consulted and the proposed new centre, although further exploration would be necessary. Most would be prepared to assist the centre by co-operating in their particular aspect of the work.

No organisation saw the new centre being responsible for finding funds to finance local community work projects.

Priority of need

Whatever the cost, high priority should be given by the statutory authorities and the charitable trusts to the needs of local community groups, since they are at present less well served than most other groups.

Proposals

*Area resource centres**

Area centres should be set up within existing organisations, not necessarily within the same kind of organisation in each area. They should be in regular contact not only with local groups but also with the national centre. They also need to operate flexibly and adaptably, so as to meet rapid changes in the local scene. It is likely that initially the greatest need for area centres will be in major conurbations, where community groups tend particularly to form themselves.

The functions of these area centres would vary according to local needs and the services already available. It is worth noting here that community groups often need help at a very early stage in their life. Functions might include:

Information   To obtain and disseminate information of practical value to local workers and members of groups, e.g. about new methods of work and successful field projects elsewhere; about housing and welfare rights, education and recreational facilities for children; information useful to ethnic and religious minorities; and details of facilities useful to a group in its own immediate neighbourhood.

Supporting services   To make available staff capable of helping groups

to use equipment such as duplicating and printing machines, tape recorders and video tapes, and display material; or to compose and lay out a community news-sheet or material for publicity;

with their book-keeping, minute-taking, correspondence and other administrative chores;

with general community work skills and local training on the spot.

The full-time staff should be small; community workers and others with particular skills or experience could be used as consultants.

Equipment   To lend from their own resources or to help in borrowing from local institutions the kinds of equipment mentioned above. Each centre should have a pool of such resources as are needed by local groups. A mobile van might help to make equipment more readily and quickly accessible.

* The Council of Social Service for Wales has recently set up an information centre for community work in Wales, with the support of the Welsh Office. It has also formed a community work forum in South Wales to meet three or four times a year, with the primary aim of bringing community workers and servicing agencies together for discussion.

Opportunities for discussion To provide facilities for meetings between members of different community groups in order to encourage discussion and the exchange of information and views.

The form of management of these area centres will depend to some extent on the type of organisation within which the centre is established. It is important that members of community groups should participate in the management of each centre, and that all those concerned with the centre should share in the decision-making. Funding should normally be a matter for the local authorities and voluntary organisations in the area (some are already beginning to provide such funds). But in order to establish the practical value of these centres it might well be necessary to obtain from central government and trusts sufficient funds to promote experimental centres, preferably in, say, two very different areas, and to publish reports on their work. The national centre might be given the practical task of establishing these two centres and might perhaps second a small staff for this purpose to the local body which gives each experimental centre a home.

National resource centre

It seems clear that a small national resource centre is needed, linking and supporting the area resource centres. Its functions should include:

Information and advisory services The centre should be linked to existing information services and should put enquirers in touch with them. It should not itself store information available elsewhere. Apart from knowing where the information is to be found, the centre would have the task of sifting relevant information and passing it to area centres in the form most suitable for local groups and for answering enquiries for information quickly. It should also try to meet the specialist needs of teachers of community work (e.g. for case studies, bibliographies and analyses of projects), in consultation with other bodies concerned. It might encourage the exchange of information and views by the issue of periodic news-sheets, but the emphasis should be on flexibility and quick response to requests. Apart from its own knowledge and expertise, the centre should be able to suggest the best sources to those seeking advice about particular aspects of community work. It should also actively support local area centres, particularly with technical aid and equipment.

Encouraging training courses of all kinds The centre would not itself attempt to provide full-time training, though it might run short courses to meet particular needs. Its concern would be both to encourage existing institutions and agencies to provide courses and to supplement the publicity given by other bodies.

Evaluation and research   There is a growing demand for evaluation of projects and for information about methods of evaluation (see chapter 5). The staff of the centre would not be expected to meet all requests for help with evaluation but should be able to suggest where and how this could be arranged, and to store or keep references to the results of evaluation. The centre should collect information about research but is unlikely to have the resources to undertake research itself. Knowledge of gaps would enable it to encourage research institutions to embark on the most fruitful work.

Facilities for discussion and the exchange of views   The national centre should have the responsibility for surveying the needs and arranging conferences, seminars or study groups as required, directly or preferably through other agencies. It should also provide the secretariat for the national forum described below.

The promotion of community work   If its expertise were firmly based on a knowledge of the practical work of area centres and local groups, the national centre should be effective in promoting initiatives and experimental work and in influencing national policy as well as community work practice.

The centre could be established either independently or under the umbrella of an existing organisation with an interest in the promotion of community work and links with other relevant agencies. It might be an advantage if the national centre served also as an area centre for its own immediate locality, in order to keep in touch with practical and local problems. In any event the centre should be a compact and operational unit with a small staff of high quality, flexible in mind and approach, having a practical knowledge of community work and an understanding of its wider implications. The centre should not duplicate resources already available.

As with area resource centres, the management and funding of a national centre presents problems. Active members of community groups and representatives from area centres should participate in management. Funding would need to be by the central government and the larger trusts.

National forums

Apart from the conferences and seminars to be arranged under the auspices of the national resource centre, there is a need for two different national forums:

An open forum concerned with all aspects of the development of community work policy and practice, meeting regularly.
Membership would be open to anyone interested or involved in

community work, including members of local community groups, and interested agencies and government departments would be invited to send representatives or observers to meetings. It is for consideration whether this particular need might be met by ACW, with whom there should be further discussion.

A closed forum in which there would be a continuing dialogue among those in the statutory and voluntary fields who have a concern for social policy and planning or for exercising influence on government, training institutions and others. In spite of the problems of selection the group would need to be limited in size. The secretariat for such a forum should be provided by the national resource centre.

National fund for community work projects

Over and above the Government Urban Programme and Community Development Project and quite apart from the funding of the area centres and national centre, a national fund is urgently needed to provide pump-priming and emergency support grants for local community work projects of all kinds. The fund might be built up from contributions by government, trusts and other voluntary sources. In the interests of co-ordination, speed and the minimum of red tape, it would be best for the fund to be administered by independent trustees.

The next step

The Community Work Group agreed to ask the Calouste Gulbenkian Foundation to study these proposals in detail and to explore the best means for their implementation.

9 Summary

Chapter 1 explains that the aim of the Community Work Group has not been to offer a comprehensive survey of community work today nor to resolve differences of opinion among its members. The foregoing chapters are the fruit of discussions, within its five sub-groups, on some current topics which seemed to call for exchange and debate from diverse viewpoints.

It follows that the strands of discussion do not, when drawn together, form a coherent design. Nevertheless it may be useful to set down in summary the main conclusions and suggestions for the future which have emerged.

A 'community-oriented' attitude of mind needs to become more widespread among policy-makers, administrators and members of relevant professions, if consultation and participation are to form part of the pattern of democracy today. Only then can there be effective communication within and between the many groupings, official or voluntary, formal or informal, amongst which both the desire to be involved in decision-making and the power to decide and to act is distributed. In some contexts, decision-makers are already more responsive to community pressures but the pace of change in this direction is both slow and uneven. However, as decisions get more complex and organisations larger and their policy-makers more remote from the people they serve, so it becomes more difficult to enable ordinary people to participate effectively in major decision-making processes.

Nevertheless, central and local government authorities and other public institutions should declare their intention to involve in decision-making, in whatever ways may be most effective, those who will be closely affected by their proposals or policies; and to explain the reasons for the final decision. A good many authorities already do this, without diminishing their elected members' responsibilities, as representatives of the people, to make decisions on their behalf; but public declarations by all would set a framework for decision-making on broad policy issues.

In order to make the process of involving people in decision-making more effective, elected members, officials and community leaders should come together to discuss practical points such as the techniques for presenting complicated proposals clearly to community groups and for seeing that the community's response has a genuine effect on decisions. Small joint working parties might well plan this, following on a declaration of intent. These discussions should help members of local communities to appreciate the extent to which the needs of one group of interests have to be weighed against those of others; and should also enable decision-makers to understand local views and desires better.

Various methods of extending opportunities for people to contribute towards policy-making and for developing the process of consultation are suggested in chapter 3. Those affected should take part in decisions about long-term policies as well as detailed development proposals; should have issues put to them in plain language and with sufficient publicity; and should be prepared to respond within reasonable time limits.

The individual 'consumer's' or employee's sense of participation in the activities especially of large and complex institutions (local authorities, public corporations, industrial and commercial undertakings, educational institutions, hospitals, etc.) is, in its own right, as important as economy, efficiency or sophistication. Unless such institutions succeed in becoming less 'remote', it is suggested that the question of scale or size ought to be reconsidered, through decentralisation or otherwise.

Community action

Factual accounts and analyses of the processes and outcome of community action in various contexts are badly needed. Practical handbooks on running groups and on relationships with official bodies, with useful factual information, would often increase the 'know-how' of such groups.

Local authorities would do well to encourage community action groups and to use their own community workers to support them, provided that the integrity and independence of the groups are respected.

Public money in limited amounts should be provided without restrictive strings for the use of community action groups. Opportunities for training should also be more widely available.

It is important to promote mutual understanding between community action groups and official and other bodies—particularly local authorities—with which they are in contact, so that these bodies may come better to recognise the contribution that the groups have to make towards a juster and more representative society.

Analysis

A framework for the analysis and evaluation of community projects is required, to encourage consistency of reporting. The information would best be centrally maintained in a 'bank' of comparable data, accessible to practitioners, teachers, researchers and policy-makers. Action research, monitored experiments, edited case studies and an abstracting service are all needed to produce materials for teaching and other purposes. A resource centre would be the most effective way of meeting these needs at the present time.

Community workers

There is increasing need for and employment of qualified community workers both in fieldwork and at inter-agency or planning levels. At the same time it is extremely important that more of those in the public service, in the 'helping professions' and working as volunteers, should remain constantly aware of the community repercussions of their work. The position of community work in the local government structure is considered at various points in this study.

Tension can easily arise between employer and employee, particularly when a community worker is concerned with militant groups. Many but not all conflicts can be resolved, given better understanding of the basis and limits of conflict. It is a good thing to encourage a variety of employing bodies in community work, so that conflict may be more productive, less a matter of 'them' and 'us'. The Community Work Group recognised, but did not attempt to reconcile, the fundamentally different points of view of those who regard conflict strategies as a means of making marginal adaptations and those who would see their purpose as bringing about fundamental shifts of power and structural changes in the social system.

There should be adequate promotion prospects for community workers in direct practice. This might entail new senior posts, in the interests of a proper career structure, for skilled and experienced workers who wish and should be encouraged to remain in neighbourhood work.

Restrictive professionalism could cramp the development of community work. On the other hand, even though the content of training may remain fluid, professional values, motives and standards of work and a degree of independence are necessary to safeguard the worker, the employer and the community.

Training

There is a real danger, in training, of divorce between teaching and practice, since methodical field studies are lacking; teachers have little time for contact with practitioners or projects; fieldwork supervision is inadequate; and there is no systematic study of the actual task in community work. Those concerned should be brought together to consult urgently on how to remedy this situation; and the remedies should be applied without delay.

There is a need for continuing study groups on curriculum content and planning, fieldwork and in-service training; also on the ethics of community intervention and on the application of the social sciences in training and practice. The Central Council for Education and Training in Social Work has a key function here.

A few full-time qualifying courses in community work should become 'centres of excellence', so as to promote effective advance in theory, practice, research and evaluation. Training is needed for the inter-agency and planning levels of community work as well as for fieldwork. Discussions under JUC auspices might help to ensure that full-time training courses at each level are inter-related.

It is to be hoped that the separation of social work courses and youth and community work courses will be reviewed. Adult education should make an increasing contribution to community work training in social work courses and social work to training in adult education courses.

Training should promote professional standards and integrity and a clear view of objectives.

Senior members of professions concerned with the community should consult together on inter-disciplinary training in community aspects of their work, including social studies. A related approach would be a closer coming together of 'public interventionists', with a view to an interprofessional approach and greater community orientation in their work.

The main needs of community work at present

A wide range of *information, advice* and *equipment* needs to be readily available, particularly to local groups, workers and teachers in community work. Information, guidance and more publicity should also be given about facilities for *training,* formal and informal and about *careers. Funds* are required both centrally and locally for these various services and for grants in support of community work projects themselves. All those concerned with community work: members of groups, fieldworkers, administrators, planners, policy-makers and teachers (whether professional or not), alike require an independent forum for discussion and exchange of views and experiences, both nationally and locally. High priority should always be given by statutory bodies and trusts to the needs of local community groups, which are often neglected at present.

Proposals for meeting these needs

A survey commissioned by the Community Work Group indicates that no single organisation at present meets the major part of any of these needs, although several are deeply involved in particular aspects. A number of these organisations favour a small national resource centre or clearing house and would be ready to work with it, according to their special experience.

Area resource centres

Centres should be set up within a suitable agency in each area, linked with a national centre. Their functions would be to disseminate the practical information and advice needed by local groups and workers; to support them by lending skilled staff and equipment and by acting as a clearing house for facilities available in the area; and to provide opportunities for discussion and exchange of views. Community groups should have a voice in managing each resource centre, which should be financed by local authorities and voluntary bodies in the area. Two demonstration centres should first be set up in very different areas, perhaps by the national centre, with funds from central government and trusts. (See p. 134 n.)

National resource centre

A compact, flexible clearing-house is proposed, with a small staff of high calibre, to link and support the area resource centres. It should on no account store or provide information or resources already available but rather be ready to refer enquirers promptly to the right source; it should process and distribute information in the most useful form and offer technical advice and equipment to area centres, teachers and others. It must be geared to responding quickly to enquiries. The centre should also encourage and publicise facilities of all kinds for community work training; stimulate evaluation and research likely to be fruitful; arrange or sponsor discussion and exchange of views; and generally promote initiatives and experiments in community work. Potentially, the centre would be well placed to influence national policy and community work practice. Active members of community groups and representatives of area centres should take part in managing the national centre, which should be financed by public and trust funds.

National forums

There is a clear need for an open forum to discuss the development of community work policy and practice, meeting regularly. Anyone with an interest in community work could participate; agencies and departments concerned would be invited to send observers. Secondly a limited group, chosen from those likely to have influence on official bodies and training institutions, should be invited to a continuing dialogue on social policy and planning, this group being serviced by the national resource centre.

National fund for projects

An independently administered fund is urgently required to provide pump-priming and emergency support grants for local community work projects of all kinds. It might be built up from government, trust and other contributions.

The next step

The Calouste Gulbenkian Foundation is invited to study these proposals further, with a view to their implementation.

Underlying issues

Three fundamental and related issues lie behind much of the preceding discussion, namely conflict strategies, the distribution of power in society and problems of effective representation in the democratic institutions of large educated populations with diverse views and needs. These issues go far beyond any consideration of community work as such, and we can do no more, in conclusion, than expose them for further discussion and analysis. Community work is essentially about social change; about the redistribution of power and scarce resources; about the inertia of large institutions; about conflicts of interest between different groups in a community; about how the activists and the inarticulate may both have a proper say in decision-making processes that affect them; and about the extent and the kind of decisions that people wish to make, or contribute to making, themselves. It is also about how it might be possible to balance institutional power with 'spontaneous' power.

Members of the Community Work Group (1970-3)†

Lord Boyle of Handsworth, PC *(Chairman) Vice-Chancellor, University of Leeds*

Mr F. J. C. Amos, CBE *Chief Planning Officer, Liverpool Corporation*

Mr John Banks *Community Development Project, Home Office (resigned October 1970)*

*Dr T. R. Batten *Reader in Community Development Studies, University of London Institute of Education (until September 1972)*

Professor Walter Birmingham *Department of Economics, University of Cape Coast, Ghana*

Dr K. Blyth *Assistant Director, The Nuffield Foundation (resigned April 1972)*

Mr G. J. Brown, OBE *HM Inspector of Schools (Informal Further Education), Scottish Education Department*

Mr Peter Brinson *Director, United Kingdom and British Commonwealth Branch, Calouste Gulbenkian Foundation*

Dr W. Burns, CB, CBE *Deputy Secretary and Chief Planner, Department of the Environment*

Mr E. D. Butterworth *Reader in Community Work, University of York*

Father Paul Byrne, OMI *Director, Shelter Housing Aid Centre*

Miss J. D. Cooper, CB *Director, Social Work Service, Department of Health and Social Security*

Mr David Corkey *Director, Community Development Centre, County Borough of Tynemouth*

Mr Frank Cousins, PC *Community Relations Commission (resigned July 1971)*

Mrs Pauline Crabbe, OBE *Secretary, Brook Advisory Centre*

Mr N. Dugdale *Permanent Secretary, Ministry of Health and Social Services, Northern Ireland (resigned October 1970)*

† Current designations are shown against those who were members in January 1973, when the Group held its last meeting. Where a member resigned earlier, the list shows the designation at that time.

Mr A. Dunbar   *Director, United Kingdom and British Commonwealth Branch, Calouste Gulbenkian Foundation (resigned December 1971)*

Mr D. R. Flockhart   *Director, Scottish Council of Social Service*

Mr John Freeman   *Community Worker, Young Volunteer Force Foundation, Stoke-on-Trent*

Mr George Goetschius *Lecturer in Social Work Studies, London School of Economics and Political Science*

*Professor J. H. Griffiths   *Department of Social Administration, New University of Ulster*

Mr Robin Guthrie   *Social Development Officer, Peterborough Development Corporation*

Mr J. E. Hannigan   *Housing Division, Ministry of Housing and Local Government (resigned February 1971)*

Mr M. J. G. Hearley   *HM Inspector of Schools (resigned August 1970)*

Mr A. C. Hetherington, CBE   *Secretary, County Councils Association*

Dr Robert Holman   *Senior Lecturer, Department of Social Administration and Social Work, University of Glasgow*

Mr Michael Holton   *Secretary, Carnegie United Kingdom Trust*

The Rt Rev. T. H. Huddleston, CR   *Bishop of Stepney (resigned October 1970)*

Mr A. R. Isserlis   *Director, Centre for Studies in Social Policy*

Miss Beti Jones   *Chief Adviser on Social Work, Social Work Services Group, Scottish Education Department*

*Mr David Jones, OBE   *Principal, National Institute for Social Work Training*

The Rev. Erastus Jones   *Warden, Ty Toronto Service Centre, Aberfan*

Professor H. A. Jones   *Department of Adult Education, University of Leicester*

*Professor R. A. B. Leaper   *Department of Sociology, University of Exeter*

*Miss E. R. Littlejohn   *Head of the Community Work Division, National Council of Social Service*

*Mr A. V. S. Lochhead, OBE   *Director of Overseas Courses, Department of Social Administration, University College of Swansea*

Mr Dudley Lofts   *Director, Local Government Training Board*

Mr D. N. Lowe, OBE   *Secretary, Carnegie United Kingdom Trust (resigned October 1970)*

Mr. F. J. Macrae, OBE, DFC   *Principal Probation Inspector, Home Office (until August 1972)*

*Mr Richard Mills   *Deputy Director, United Kingdom and British Commonwealth Branch, Calouste Gulbenkian Foundation*

Dr F. W. Milson   *Head of Youth & Community Service Section, Westhill College of Education*

Mr O. H. Morris   *Assistant Secretary, Community Health Division, Welsh Office (resigned October 1970)*

Mr Dipak Nandy   *Director, Runnymede Trust*

Mr John O'Malley   *Director, Community Development Project, London Borough of Newham*

Mr. P. R. Odgers, CB, MBE   *Cabinet Office (resigned September 1971)*

Mr J. K. Owens   *Director, National Council of Social Service*

Lady Plowden   *(resigned May 1971)*

Mr Peter Polish   *Projects Director, Community Development Trust*

Mr H. R. Poole   *Secretary, Liverpool Council of Social Service*

Mr A. R. G. Prosser, CMG, MBE   *Adviser on Social Development, Overseas Development Administration, Foreign and Commonwealth Office*

Mr C. M. Regan   *Under-Secretary, Department of Health and Social Security*

Mr R. A. Richardson   *HM Inspector of Schools*

Mr A. F. Robinson   *Lecturer in Sociology, North East Essex Technical College and School of Art*

Miss E. L. Sewell, OBE   *Administrative Officer, Study Group on Training for Community Work, 1967–8*

The Rev. G. M. Shaw   *Secretary, Crossroads Youth and Community Service Association, Glasgow*

Miss A. M. Sheridan   *Deputy Director, Social Work Service, Department of Health and Social Security*

Dr C. S. Smith   *Director of Studies, Social Policy and Social Administration, Civil Service College*

*Mrs Muriel Smith, MBE   *Adviser to the Community Development Project, Home Office*

Professor J. C. Spencer   *Department of Social Administration, University of Edinburgh*

Mr J. C. Swaffield, CBE   *Secretary, Association of Municipal Corporations (resigned December 1972)*

*Professor D. F. Swift   *Faculty of Educational Studies, The Open University (resigned October 1970)*

Mr W. E. K. Taylor   *Community Worker, Greenwich Community Project*

Miss Patricia Thomas   *Assistant Director, The Nuffield Foundation*

Mr L. E. Waddilove   *Director, Joseph Rowntree Memorial Trust (resigned October 1970)*

*Professor E. A. O. G. Wedell   *(Vice-Chairman)   Department of Adult Education, University of Manchester*

Mr Macdonald Wilkinson   *Area Youth and Community Service Officer, Midlothian Education Committee, Livingston New Town*

Appendix 1

Application of the framework for analysis to a shopping expedition*

(See chapter 5, p. 71)

1 *Background*

The Browns, a family of four, live in a suburb of Northtown about a mile from the town centre. Mrs Brown usually shops in the town centre on Friday, market day, because she likes to have the larder full for the weekend and finds the market gives good value.

2 *Reasons for the initiative*

On 13 April Mrs Brown needed to buy food and certain household goods. The presence and extent of the need was known by the housewife because of

2.1 her previous experience of the amount consumed by her family in a week,
2.2 a check on the level of stocks in the larder,
2.3 requests from the family for particular foods to be bought.

The situation was appreciated by Mr Brown, although he was not interested in the details.

3 *Objectives*

3.1 to buy a week's supply of dry goods, meat and vegetables for two days and new shoes for daughter, Jane,
3.2 to be home again by 4 pm to prepare Mr Brown's tea.

Mrs Brown intended to achieve both objectives but, if necessary, would sacrifice the shoes first. Jane was more concerned with getting the shoes. The achievement of objective 3.1 could be measured against Mrs Brown's shopping list.

5 *Organisation, policies and principles*

Organisation The Brown family consists of Mr and Mrs Brown, a son aged seven and a daughter aged three. Mr Brown works for a local insurance

* Sections are numbered in accordance with the framework itself, so that the numbering is not always continnous.

firm and Master Brown attends a local school. Mrs Brown and her daughter spend Thursdays with Mrs Brown's mother who lives in the next street.

Policies   The Brown family always walk in preference to travelling by bus, provided the weather is fine. This was mutually agreed between Mr and Mrs Brown several years ago.

Principles   The Browns consider walking is a healthy activity. They also set great store by thrift.

6   *Intended action*

Mrs Brown intended to walk, with Jane in her push chair, first to the market and then to the shoe shop. Walking round the market comparing prices was an essential part of the routine.
She anticipated difficulty in finding good-quality, well-fitting shoes which she could afford.

7   *Resources*

Mrs Brown, a fit and experienced housewife, perfectly capable of undertaking the task efficiently. Time $1\frac{1}{2}$ hours.

Push chair for transporting the child.

£5 from the housekeeping money supplied by Mr Brown.

8   *Action*

2.30 pm   set out as planned.

2.50 pm   reach market—Jane wanders away and mother spends about ten minutes searching for her.

3.10 pm   finds child, hurriedly finishes food shopping and proceeds to shoe shop which is busy.

3.30 pm   shoes bought, now raining, so Mrs Brown and Jane catch a bus. Mrs Brown checks shopping list on the bus and realises she has forgotten the potatoes.

3.50 pm   arrive home.

9   *Development*

Change in methods—bus journey home—resources depleted by £4·90.

10   *Process analysis*

Mrs Brown's failure to buy any potatoes was almost certainly due to the temporary loss of her daughter. It was caused initially by her anxiety and her determination about the expedition. Her search for Jane then caused her to fall ten minutes behind schedule, and this, in turn, followed by the rain, caused her further anxiety, so that she omitted to check her shopping list until it was too late to buy any potatoes.

11 *Evaluation*

Mrs Brown achieved her objectives except for buying potatoes. Resources were adequate.

Unforeseen achievement—Jane learnt not to let go of her mother's hand in a crowded place.

Lessons for similar projects in the future:

11.1 shoes are increasing in price—allow more resources in future.
11.2 always consult shopping list before leaving market.

Appendix 2

A case study of the Bentilee Valley Projects Committee
An exercise in public participation*

(See chapter 5, p. 71) (Written in May 1972)

Introduction

This case study was written to test the framework for analysis produced by the Community Work Group in their work on the analysis of projects. It examines the Bentilee Valley Projects Committee half-way through its work. The study was carried out by a member of the Young Volunteer Force (YVF) team concerned in the project, a community worker with considerable experience.

1 *Background*

Bentilee is a large housing estate in Stoke-on-Trent which was built by the Council in the early 1950s. Development took place on farm land in the east of the City about two miles from the centre and local authority offices. The estate is completely surrounded by remaining farm land and this produces a feeling of isolation among the residents and a peculiar mixture of urban and rural existence. The houses are solid but drab, being of the normal red brick semi-detached construction. The estate is long and narrow (one and a half miles long and about half a mile wide), and the population numbers 15,000. Three characterless roads run lengthways through the estate with houses numbering up to 700. While local shopping is adequate, general amenities are uniform—mainly working men's clubs, pubs and some welfare facilities. There is also a large community centre. The estate has a low reputation in other parts of the City (some call it Dodge City).

The relationship between many local people and the Council has been tense for much of the history of the estate. One bone of contention has been the Brook that runs through the middle of the estate, which has been left completely derelict despite being the designated public open space. Promises to renovate this land have been made by the Council but have never materialised. The total area of ground involved is 63 acres and the majority of the population live within walking distance of the area.

In the early part of 1970, a YVF team of two workers took premises in the middle of the local shopping centre. For many reasons they saw their brief as involving the whole community and not just young people. Thus

---

* Sections are numbered in accordance with the framework for analysis; certain items in the framework are not covered in the study, so that the numbering is not always continuous.

they had been working in the area for over a year before this project commenced and so were reasonably well established.

2 *Reasons for the initiative*

2.1 *Opportunities and problems*

2.1.1 *As seen by those affected* The majority of Bentilee residents are affected. Most feelings about the Brook are negative, being represented by statements like 'the Brook is infested by rats', 'it's a place people dump rubbish', 'the Brook is filthy', and 'in winter you can't get across it.' This last statement comes particularly from the elderly. Some of the stories about the Brook, particularly the ones about the level of pollution, are in my opinion true, but all stories about the Brook are believed by local people. Some use is made of the area for kick-about football and taking dogs for walks, and so there is a basic desire and need to use this piece of land. A further problem is that local people do not believe that any change will occur in the state of the Brook. This follows from the fact that the Council have promised to revamp the area on several occasions. Nothing has so far been done.

2.1.2 *As seen by those responsible* By 'responsible' I understand those people, organisations or groups which have some power in relation to this area of land. These are:

The Labour Party Since this project is involved in the allocation of resources political groups are obviously important. The Labour Party is the dominant party both locally in Bentilee and in the City where they have a three to one majority on the City Council. Thus they are the only relevant political party in this case study. The Ward Labour Party has, of course, been aware of local people's feelings about the Brook. They have attempted to get the necessary finance allocated on numerous occasions, but until recently have failed. The refusal of the Labour-controlled Council to allocate funds led to the resignation of one of the Bentilee councillors in 1966.

The relationship between the Ward Labour Party and the Central, City-based Labour Group is obviously important in determining the power of the Ward Labour Party and the policies that it can hope to get implemented. It would be naive to suggest that the policies of the Ward Labour Party are always accepted by the Central Labour Group. It is also clear that the departments of the City Council have considerable influence over the implementation of proposals.

The Planning Department This Department has grown in strength over the past few years, largely because Stoke-on-Trent has an extensive reclamation programme. In line with the planning profession generally the professional staff of this department are interested in ideas of participation. Because of the history of conflict over the Brook, they are aware of the crucial nature of the Brook for Bentilee people. Some planners are also slightly embarrassed by the way that the Bentilee community has developed. The planners had expected that it would be a more attractive place than it has turned out in practice.

The Parks Department   This department has owned the Bentilee Valley for a long period of time and has been attacked on numerous occasions by Bentilee residents because of inactivity. For many reasons it has failed to secure the necessary resources to reclaim the Brook. It is not one of the major City departments and so is unable to get as many resources as it needs. It is generally interested in fairly traditional ideas of parks provision and recreational provision.

The Young Volunteer Force   This organisation, being the authors of this report, saw the reclamation of the Brook as a chance to generate a major debate about decisions on the environment of Bentilee. Being a community work agency it was concerned to ensure that a large number of people discussed future developments fully.

The Harold Clowes Community Association   This Association has close links with the Ward Labour Party and is primarily concerned with managing a large community centre. Thus it has not had as much effect on the scheme as might be expected.

2.1.3   *As seen by outsiders—people living outside Bentilee*   There will be little opposition to this scheme from people living outside Bentilee because much of the money does not in fact come from the Stoke ratepayer. The government will pay 75 per cent of the cost. There is some feeling that Bentilee asks for more resources than other areas and this is one potential influence.

Residents of the estate who never use the Brook   There are some people who will not use the Brook area. Generally their view will be that while the proposal is irrelevant to their needs they are pleased to see the area cleaned up.

Councillors from other wards   Those in positions of power concerned with Planning and Parks Departments will be pleased to see this scheme starting because it will remove a major source of discontent.

2.2   *Values identifiable in groups and individuals*

Local residents   It is fair to say that the Potteries people are a warm and gentle people. They are fairly parochial and generally accept existing leadership structures.

Parks Department   Generally they feel that they are a poor relation among the City Departments and tend to do things that have already been tried. As with many local authority departments they would like to expand their field of operations.

Planning Department   In line with the planning profession generally they are interested in public participation, but at the same time they are aware of the pressures on them from the elected representatives to make decisions reasonably quickly. They see the reclamation programme as an area where they can become experienced in participation without holding up some other major schemes.

Young Volunteer Force The YVF are committed to community work principles but realise that it is important to achieve something reasonably quickly. Prepared to take a leadership role should it be required.

Bentilee Valley Projects Committee This developed into a group as the project continued and some incidents in its development will be discussed later.

3 Objectives

3.1 General objectives

a. To tidy up the Brook so that it would become a suitable place for people to come and use for their leisure. This would include getting the right kind of amenity in the correct place on the estate.
b. To involve more local residents in playing a part in decisions affecting the estate. This would include providing residents with the right kind of information and learning situation so that they can make informed decisions.
c. To experiment in methods of participation in planning.

3.2 Specific targets or short-term objectives

a. There were many groups wanting specific amenities. The local football team wanted a football pitch. The local Senior Citizens' Association wanted a park which would be acceptable to old people.
b. There were specific measures taken to inform more people about the decisions that were being made. This included starting a local paper which discussed issues raised by the Brook projects.
There was a procedure for obtaining news from local people about the proposals. This included holding public meetings and mounting an exhibition by the schools on the theme of Bentilee and the environment.

3.3 Priorities

Different priorities exist in different groups and this has led to conflict on occasions. One dilemma has been how much time consultation should take.
How much time should be spent in obtaining local people's views and their commitment to the proposed changes in the Brook area? Some members of the more established groups in the community like the Ward Labour Party wanted brief involvement of other local people, taking the form of one public meeting. Other groups like the YVF wanted greater stress on involving more people in the required decision-making.

5 Policies

5.1 Existing policies of the Water Board
They have certain policies about the flow of water which affect the Brook proposal.
5.2 Planning Department
They have no defined policy on public participation as it is changing at the present time. They are of

course committed to referring all major decisions to the elected representatives.

5.3   *Parks Department*   The scheme must look reasonably tidy and be suitable for easy upkeep. Other statements about policies have already been made. (It should be noticed that statements on policies are difficult to obtain as sometimes they are not stated or specified).

6   *Intended action*

Planning of strategy   Strategy is planned by informal groups on the estate, being the ones already mentioned. Methods of achieving goals are generally those of consensus and of producing legitimate arguments.

7   *Resources*

7.1   *Time available*   The community worker employed by the YVF spends about a quarter of his time on this project. Normal amounts of time are spent by the City officials from the Parks, Highways and Planning Departments. They are, however, prepared to spend some extra time on evening meetings with the public. It is difficult to estimate the amount of time that has been given by people in a voluntary capacity but at least a dozen meetings have been held concerning this project.

7.2   *Money*   About £90,000 is available to do the actual physical work in reclaiming the area. This scheme comes under the government reclamation scheme and so 75 per cent of the cost is borne by the government. Small sums have been provided locally for the participation exercise and the administrative costs involved. The sums involved are about £25 which have come from local organisations.

7.3   *Land*   63 acres of land are available for this project.

7.4   *Skills*   Since the project has been a genuine partnership between the City Council and local residents in the Bentilee Valley Projects Committee the skills of the local authority have been available to the project. This includes planning and layout skills. Community work skills and contacts were provided by the YVF and since many people on the Committee had experience of committee procedures there were skills in this direction. There was also a high degree of knowledge about the local political situation. It should be noted that when some minor conflict existed between the planning department and the local group the possibility of obtaining skills from elsewhere was explored. As it turned out this was not required but channels were being opened by the community workers to the University and elsewhere.

7.5   *Organisation structure and relationships: formal and informal workings—Bentilee Valley Projects Committee*   This Committee was formed to discuss and make recommendations concerning the Brook. It is a representative committee of all major organisations on the estate. The chairman is the chairman of the local Ward Labour Party and the secretary is the community worker employed by the YVF. It meets about once a month and all major business is conducted at these meetings. Planners and representatives of the Parks Department are invited to some of the meetings but they are not present as a matter of course.

Local councillors are also invited but have not attended every meeting. Representatives do not seem to have been reporting back to their committees or organisations, and so the BVPC has established an identity of its own. The 'guts' of the organisation is about three or four people who have fairly good informal links. These people are the chairman, the secretary and a man involved with youth activities who is on the fringe of the political structure. One important organisation that does affect what BVPC can do is the Labour Party. The group has some links with the Labour Party and therefore is careful about its relationship with the Council. There are good informal links between the community worker and the planner in charge of the planning aspects of the project.

8 *Action*

This section is laid out in time sequence.

Aug. 1971	A Planning Department official takes a man from the Department of Environment around the Brook area. They agree to classify it as derelict.
29.9.71	Ward Labour Party hears that Brook is likely to be reclaimed and calls for public meeting. Eighty people attend (which is unusually high for the estate) and participation is mentioned.
1.10.71	Worker from YVF discusses situation with Ward Labour Party.
12.10.71	Ward Labour Party meeting votes to make the project of consulting people independent of the Labour Party.
15.10.71	Planner meets YVF worker and expresses interest and willingness to give time to participation.
Nov. 1971	75 per cent Government grant confirmed.
23.11.71	Bentilee Valley Projects Committee inaugurated. Twenty-three people present representing fifteen local bodies and local councillors.
7.12.71	Second meeting of the BVPC—twenty-seven people present. Two working parties are set up discussing sport and play, parks and landscaping. Outline for future action proposed.
3.1.72	First newsletter distributed to local residents explaining what is happening. This was an attempt to inform more people, so that they could have a view on the project.
4.1.72	Fourth meeting of the BVPC with the Planning Department represented. Planner indicates that no firm plans have been formalised by his Department but adds that this meeting closes consultation with BVPC. Mild objections raised. Planner outlines Planning Department schedule. Working parties report.
14.1.72	Letter to Planning Department stating that their schedule does not allow for full participation and proposing alternative time schedule.
21.1.72	YVF have meeting with an adviser on planning.
25.1.72	Letter to all schools requesting help with exhibition on theme 'Bentilee, Past, Present and Future'.

25.1.72	BVPC hold public meeting. Forty people present including some new faces. Thoughts of working parties expressed. Need for continued development and maintenance after the initial reclamation stressed.
30.1.72	Second newsletter goes out.
4.2.72	YVF representative meets with local schools to discuss proposed exhibition.
15.2.72	At BVPC meeting revised time schedule is accepted by Planning Department. Specific recommendations are being made by the working parties.
29.2.72	Exhibition on the scheme is opened in the YVF shop. (This is a different exhibition to the one on 'Bentilee Past, Present and Future' which will be prepared by the schools.)
29.2.72	Group of local adults meet to discuss newsletter.
Mid-March 1972	Third newsletter produced by local group with help of YVF worker. Covers issues not only referring to the Brook but of general local interest.
28.3.72	BVPC meeting. Letter received from a group of residents in the south of the estate asking for information about proposals for their area. (This group felt that they were not being fully consulted.) More discussion on follow-up of scheme including discussion of overall representative structures of the estate. Also discussion of maintaining the Brook area once the reclamation is completed. Plans agreed for public meetings to be held in working men's clubs and some pubs to inform people about the scheme. Master plan prepared by Planning and Parks Department submitted to local residents. Being considered at the present time by BVPC but embodies the bulk of their recommendations.

10 *Process analysis*

While it is impossible to detail all things happening in this project there were probably three key moments in its development from the community work standpoint. These incidents were:

10.1 The decision of the Ward Labour Party to make the project of consulting local people independent of the Labour Party. If the Labour Party had retained control of this project several results would have followed. It is quite likely that the public would not have heard nearly so much about the project. This follows from the fact that this would have been only one item on the Labour Party agenda, as well as the likelihood that the Ward Party would have wished to have the bulk of discussion within its own membership. Thus involvement of other organisations would have been lower and consultation of the general public less. Since there is some identification of the Ward Labour Party with the Council, and since some local people feel that the Council have not honoured all the promises on the Brook, it is likely that people would be less willing to participate in a Labour Party exercise. There would also be problems for an organisation like YVF in taking part in a politically backed exercise.

10.2   The second key event was a meeting of the BVPC on 4.1.72. At this meeting a senior planner informed the BVPC of the time schedule, which did not allow the BVPC to prepare a reasoned case for the Planning Department. The timing of the schedule was dictated by procedural considerations in the Planning Department and the timing of Council committees and the meeting of the full Council. The question of time is of crucial importance in participation, because one legitimate worry is that discussion could take place for years and no decisions ever be made. Thus a compromise is usually required. By challenging the time schedule of the Planning Department and the Parks Department and getting the revised proposal accepted, this project became a true partnership between local residents and the planners. If the revised schedule had not been accepted participation would have been negligible. In a partnership of this type planners need to be very sensitive to local people's attitudes. In general in Stoke, high status is placed on the words of educated professionals and, on occasions, this needs to be challenged.

10.3   The third key incident occurred on 28.3.72. A letter was written by a group of residents living in the south of the estate requesting information. The BVPC interpreted this letter as a challenge to their authority in speaking for the whole of the estate. They had become an established group and felt that this letter did not acknowledge their right to represent local people's views on the Brook. Part of the reason for this attitude was the knowledge that a person with extreme political views was connected with the letter.

11   *Results and evaluation*

Although the project is not yet complete it seems likely that the Brook will be reclaimed, in line with the wishes of the Bentilee Valley Project Committee. Thus objective (a) is likely to be achieved. In terms of the less concrete goals mentioned in objective (b) it is fair to say that more people have a better knowledge of the workings of local government. Further than that it is difficult to say at this stage, and a complete evaluation will have to await the completion of the project. Nevertheless there is solid achievement in terms of the flow of information and growing potential for change. This is seen particularly in terms of interest in a neighbourhood council and in ensuring that the reclamation scheme is followed up. This may include the consideration of further amenities in the Brook area, particularly those that can be constructed by local labour. Another result is that there is a greater communication between the schools and community groups on the estate. The growth of the newsletter into a full community newspaper is another solid achievement.

Appendix 3

Analysis of information received from certain educational institutions, June 1972

(See chapter 7, p. 106)

Differing views about the teaching of community work

1   The assumptions that community work is desirable, feasible, identifiable and teachable are widespread, but not universal. The staff of ten institutions expressed a variety of views of which the following are examples:

'We are not convinced that preparation for community work should be separate from other aspects of social work.'

'Community work does not have a direct bearing on individual cases and therefore could not be regarded as a kind of social work intervention. The boundary between community work and social work is not easy to define and there is much overlap.'

'In our view community work contains a range of activities all of which are an essential part (however small) of the wide task of any social worker who hopes to render an effective service . . . Differences in practice in casework, group work, residential work and community work are a matter of emphasis rather than a matter of the alteration of basic principle.'

'I would not claim that the teaching we provide equips the student with any degree of competence as a group worker or a community worker. Nor would I wish to do so. Unlike many courses, some of which have only recently jumped on the community work bandwaggon, we have from our inception made every effort to broaden the perspectives of the potential social caseworker.'

'In general it is felt that community work should be an integral part of a training course, to give a balanced approach and follow a middle line policy.'

'All staff are very doubtful whether community work should be taught as a subject in itself.'

'I have a very unscientific idea that successful community work depends upon a peculiar kind of genius and that formalisation often leads only to its exclusion.'

'The staff are concerned to include community work as an integral part of the course rather than as a separate entity.'

'It has been agreed that there is no agreed framework of formal learning relevant to the exploratory professions such as community and youth work, as distinct from the established professions . . . Little is known as yet which would help us to define a body of theoretical knowledge for community and youth work.'

'We find it increasingly difficult to make any valid distinction between social group work and community work method. Experience suggests that social group work is the generic skill for all sorts of community work.'

2 The views quoted above do not mean that these universities, poly-technics or colleges provide no teaching in community work. In fact they all except one do so. Apart from those who question whether it is appropriate to attempt to teach community work as a separate subject or method of social work, staff in six institutions regard community work teaching, however desirable, as difficult or impossible to include in the length of their existing courses, for the following reasons:

a. Concern was expressed about the pressure on students and the range of understanding and skill expected of them in a two-year social work course. A third year was regarded as desirable;
b. It was the view of staff that they could not provide in two years a generic course that brought students to an adequate level of practice in all methods of social work;
c. It was said that one year was too brief to do all that one would like;
d. The social work staff felt strongly that there was a limit to what could be offered in a two-year basic course (there is no teaching in community work at this institution at the present time);
e. The tutors to the social work course thought it important that students should be familiar with group and community work; but in a one-year course it was only possible to specialise in the teaching of one social work method; and social casework was the principal one taught;
f. One respondent said that there was no time in a one-year course to build up a substantial amount of teaching in community work. The existing course is to be extended to two years in 1973 when community work teaching will be expanded.

Theoretical teaching

3 The information provided about theoretical teaching in community work reveals the following variations in the length of lecture courses or seminars:

	Members of the JUC	Other social work courses recognised by the CCETSW
1 to 3 lectures or seminars	3	2
4 to 6 lectures or seminars	1	6
7 to 10 lectures or seminars	4	2
1 term lectures or seminars	5	2
2 terms lectures or seminars	3	1
1 year lectures or seminars	3	2
Related material provided in other lecture courses	7	5
Total	26	20

4   The courses or seminars above are of three kinds: on community work as such; including but not confined to material on community work— for example, courses on 'Principles and Practice of Social Work'; or primarily on more general subjects, only touching on community work as a small part of the whole—for example, general sociology or social administration lectures. There are thirty-two of the first of these three kinds of courses, nine of the second and seven of the third. These forty-eight courses exceed the forty-six institutions providing such teaching because there is more than one course at two of them.

5   These figures show that where teaching in community work is given, the majority of courses are designed specifically for that purpose. This must be read with caution, however, as it may suggest that more teaching is given in community work than is in fact the case. As is clear from the table above, five of the courses consist of one to three lectures or seminars only and seven of four to six only. In so short a duration of time teaching in depth is not possible. Nevertheless, the current trend seems to be for community work to be taught in its own right and not as an appendage to some other subject.

6   In all, thirty-eight of the universities, polytechnics or colleges of further education which are members of the JUC or have other courses recognised by the CCETSW sent copies of syllabi of lectures or seminars in community work; or outlined in letters the aspects of community work that were included in their teaching. Seven others referred to teaching community work but made no mention, either in syllabi or letters, of the content of the teaching. One provides only practical experience and no theoretical teaching. The aspects of community work set out in syllabi or letters were outlined or worded in various ways and a list of very considerable length would be necessary if each aspect mentioned were to be included separately. To reduce the material to manageable proportions, twenty main headings, or aspects of community work, are listed in the following table, showing the numbers in the total of thirty-eight institutions concerned which include any given aspect in teaching community work.

7   The following headings are arranged in what appears to be a logical order, not according to the weight given to them in any given course. The order does not necessarily bear any relation to the order of material included in any of the syllabi themselves.

Aspect of community work	Institutions including this aspect in a lecture course or seminar	
	(No.)	(%)
1 The meaning, nature, or structure of 'community'	16	42
2 Definition of the terms community work, action, development, organisation	14	37
3 The historical background, origins or development of community work	7	18
4 The rationale, values, justification or purpose of community work	12	32

Aspect of community work	Institutions including this aspect in a lecture course or seminar	
	(No.)	(%)
5 Similarities or differences between community work and other methods of social work	16	42
6 The planning or organisation of community work	15	39
7 Professionals and professionalism in community work	17	45
8 Roles, skills, strategies, tactics or techniques of community work or workers	20	53
9 'Relationships' in a group or community	8	21
10 The identification of needs or problems in a community	13	34
11 Social change or social action	30	79
12 Pressure groups and other means of intervention in community work	31	82
13 Conflict, contest and consensus	25	66
14 Power or social control	16	42
15 Consumer or community participation	14	37
16 Voluntary organisations and voluntary workers in community work	8	21
17 Community leaders and leadership	9	24
18 Politics or political implications of community work	4	11
19 Community care	3	8
20 Social surveys and social research	5	13

Aspects mentioned by less than three institutions: race relations, 2; urban and rural differences, 2; welfare rights, 1; community work in other countries, 2.

8 One thing stands out above all else in the above analysis. Whereas twenty aspects of community work are identified as taught by the institutions as a whole, only four aspects are taught by more than half of them. Even if it is assumed that some syllabi or letters did not do justice to the content of the courses they referred to, and that in fact more is included than was apparent, it still seems that the content of teaching varies considerably from one course to another. This is to be expected in comparisons between a specialist course or option in community work and another which only gives three or four lectures or seminars in the subject, but all the differences seen above cannot be explained in this way.

9 Seventeen of the thirty-eight respondents who sent information about the content of their teaching also sent copies of bibliographies provided for their students. The number of books, reports or articles included varies from sixty or more to ten or less. For most courses, the number ranged between thirteen and thirty-four. There appears to be no consensus as to what constitutes reasonable reading expectations or capacities of students. One student, in his own evaluation of his fieldwork placement, said: 'I found the suggested reading overwhelming'. The list contained sixty items.

10   Ten respondents referred to the use of case studies, models or films as teaching material. One course also uses what was called a syndicate exercise or class game designed to bring out some of the problems of community work. It may well be that case studies or similar teaching material are used in other courses but were not mentioned in the information sent.

Fieldwork

11   It is difficult to sum up accurately the number or extent of fieldwork placements in community work, whether required or optional for students, as the information was given in so varied a form of words and sometimes in a vague and confusing way. But in so far as it can be tabulated the position is as follows:

	JUC members
No community fieldwork placements	8
1 placement (length unspecified)	4
2 placements (length unspecified)	1
2 or 2½ days a week (no. of weeks unspecified)	3
6 or 7 weeks	2
4 to 6 months	4
For 'some' students (length unspecified)	6
Total	28

	Other social work courses recognised by the CCETSW
No community fieldwork placements	8
No mention of fieldwork one way or the other	3
2 to 4 days a week (no. of weeks unspecified)	3
2 weeks	1
2 months	2
For 'some' students (length unspecified)	5
Total	22

These figures show that about one-third of the courses teaching community work apparently make no provision for fieldwork placements in community work. Where they exist, the nature of the placements and the agencies used vary enormously. They include councils of social service, 'community action projects', 'community projects', community centres, community associations, family advice centres, family service units, settlements, local authority housing and social services departments, tenants' associations, tenants' action groups, new town development corporations, neighbourhood associations or councils, adventure playgroups, pre-school playgroups, youth or community work on housing estates or in an education department, and community relations work.

12   It is clear from this variety that what is regarded as community work for the purpose of fieldwork placements extends over a wide spectrum. In some instances it may either be group work or else a new community project, for example in adventure playgroups, pre-school playgroups,

social services departments or family service units. Awareness of the confusion or possible confusion here is shown in a remark by an American staff member of a two-year social work course who commented that there had not been a sufficient distinction in the course between group work and community work. Indeed sometimes no distinction is to be seen. This college is one of three institutions whose social work course had gained from direct experience in the United States or from American teachers, the other two being universities. Visits of observation, as distinct from field-work placements, are mentioned by only six institutions, although in two or three instances the fieldwork arranged is described more as a period of extended observation than as an opportunity for active participation in community work.

13   The nature of fieldwork included in the seven youth and community work courses for which information was received is not spelt out in any detail. One arranges a five-week period of concentrated practical work with a trained person, two periods of two sessions a week in the field in term time and residential work in the vacation in 'appropriate community agencies'. Another provides weekly placements during two terms in the first year, six weeks in the third term and a block placement of unspecified length in the second year. Yet another arranges 'short commitments of various kinds' in the first year during the second term and 'several long-term placements of two or three sessions a week as unpaid normal part-timers.' This course is not in a position to ask for supervision.

14   One post-graduate course devotes one-third of its time to supervised practical work with weekly and block placements in councils of social service, tenants' associations and similar organisations. It is said to be difficult to find projects which combine community participation and professional skills in the supervision of students. In another course fieldwork consists of two terms of 'applied studies placements with a wide range of experience giving opportunities for community work'; yet another course includes a three-month placement of an unspecified nature.

15   Of the community development courses in adult education depart-ments, one arranges fieldwork but of an unspecified nature or length. To find specific community development placements is said to be a problem. Another includes no fieldwork as all its students are said to be experienced already. A third with an option in adult and community education said that 'emphasis was placed on practical work'.

16   A CNAA sociology degree course with an option in community work includes three terms in fieldwork placements, 'giving experience of different types of community work both in an administrative setting and in a local neighbourhood setting'.

17   Some fifteen to twenty courses require or arrange for students to take part in community work projects or special studies of various kinds; some on an individual, some on a group basis. The precise number is uncertain, since what is or what is not a project worthy of the name is not always made clear. In so far as the work might properly be called a project, it includes studies in depth of some aspect of the work of the agency in which fieldwork was undertaken: a questionnaire survey of delinquency; surveys of social need or social studies of a given area; studies of a socially vulnerable group, for example the homeless; a social study of a school;

and what were simply called 'exercises', 'projects' or 'research' of an unidentified nature. Where students are involved in a local community, as in some of the projects outlined, care needs to be taken not to leave the community bereft at the end of the vacation, term or course when the students depart. This is appreciated and in one course it is said that care is taken to avoid the 'use' of a community group in unacceptable ways. In another however it is said:

> 'There are difficulties because our students are only in the field one day a week and this occurs only during term time. Consequently some of the activities (in the project) collapse during the students' absence and particularly at the end of the long summer break a good deal of work is involved in reviving these activities. Although this may appear destructive, the work which our students are doing is work which would otherwise not be done, so that we feel that, over all, there is benefit to the community even though this is not ideal.'

18   The limitations and difficulties relating to community work in professional social work education include the varied quality of the placements, the supervision of students, and the different types of supervision in the less clearly defined situations which many community work placements offer. The importance of close liaison between tutor and supervisor is underlined. There is also the fact that sometimes community workers are seen by students to have a monopoly of radicalism and they split off community work from their social work methods-learning generally. This is said to reflect a general current issue which must be dealt with in professional teaching.

19   Inter-agency co-ordination is regarded as an important aspect of community work and also developing resources in finding suitable student projects. Concurrent placements are difficult in community settings as relevant meetings occur when students are away and students find it difficult to make meaningful connections with callers at neighbourhood centres when they are only there half the week. It is said to be a delicate task teaching or helping students to appreciate the source of the frustration of community workers who are facing many difficulties in the development of their professional activities. Problems include the pressure of time for supervisors in devising a reasonable work-load for students and for students in planning their work effectively; the conflict between giving breadth of experience and depth; confusion on the part of students in the unstructured nature of community work agencies and when they are expected to take the initiative in a situation where they are students; the amount of time taken up in supervision and the necessity for close liaison to ensure that students cannot 'play off' supervisors if there is no close co-operation between them; and the necessity for supervisors to carry on work begun but left by students before it is completed.

20   The lack of training of supervisors in community work causes considerable anxiety and the planning of placements is seen to need more consideration. 'Observation work can too easily be given because it is difficult to find suitable projects in which students can take some responsibility.'

21   In one course, supervisors' reports on community work students are

intended to include expressions of opinion on ten aptitudes, plus fourteen administrative abilities, plus twelve organisational abilities, plus relationships with seven different kinds of people in twenty different ways, plus thirteen aspects of helping skills, plus comments on regularity, punctuality and attendance, and the student's general potential for community work. Papers were sent from another course with a community work option about the suggested content of supervisors' reports on the performance of students in community fieldwork placements; these set out eight heads as a guide for group contact recording sheets, eight heads for individual interview recording sheets and thirteen heads for a written placement report on students.

Teaching problems

22   A number of problems in the teaching of community work, whether in theory or practice, were referred to and the extracts from the material sent which follow indicate their nature and significance. Only comments based on actual experience are included.

'In our view it is imperative that students should be supervised in their community work placements by someone who is trained and experienced in this form of social work. It does not follow, and in many respects may be illogical, that this person should be a professionally trained caseworker. We have been careful to ensure that the students would be given a demanding and informed period of training in the various aspects of community work carried by agencies used for fieldwork. This is the yardstick for our choice and not the fact that particular supervisors from these agencies were once trained in casework.'

'We are finding that a considerable amount of work needs to be done in defining skills in community work placements in order to make them constructive training agencies for students.'

'In the Diploma in Social Work it does not prove necessary to make any alteration in width or depth to the existing concepts of the principles and practice of social work in order to accommodate the basic principles of community work. We take into account the fact that differing demands may appropriately be made of social workers at differing stages of their development and practice and believe that identification of the resultant levels of work is a task needing clarification from social work education in the near future. In educating students to practise as comfortably and efficiently as possible in conditions of change it is usually helpful to distinguish appropriate levels of competence. We aim at securing community work supervision from people qualified at an applied social studies course level but recognising that the employment of such people may take time, we are contemplating a plan whereby a staff member will convene a group discussion with students placed in a community work agency, together with the community work supervisor.'

'Two students in community work placements faced difficulties in the unstructured nature of the placements and found it hard to develop a role for themselves. They felt concern about the degree of involvement desirable as they knew that the placement was only temporary. They felt it wrong to become too deeply involved, only to withdraw. For a time the placements were observational only and though there was opportunity later for some independent action, concern about the balance of observation and action remained.'

'We were faced with the usual problem of how to evaluate the performance of students in community work placements. The total group of supervisors decided that many of the normal criteria were applicable but in addition they clarified what they were looking for.'

'There have been students who felt during their community work placement that they had not learned very much from the work they had done. Later in the course they were able to see that there were benefits which they absorbed and took on into their further placements.'

'There needs to be further clarification as to the acceptability, length, type, and so on, of community placements on a first degree course which would still enable students to be considered and accepted for professional training. As it was, a number of students took traditional social work placements on their first degree course when they might have welcomed wider experience in the community.'

'One of the difficulties in the field of community work is the lack of expertise in supervision. This differs somewhat from the social work agencies where professional supervision was an in-built part of the fabric. However, new organisations were found and were generally very willing to co-operate and provide a thorough programme. The students found the experience very worthwhile. One is largely concerned with an initiating process; as even with proven organisations to which one returns, new supervisors arrive. This does make the question of recognition more difficult. In the last two years however more supervisory experience has been built up, with further demands being made for community work placements; and there are now some organisations with very experienced supervisors. Nevertheless, with voluntary bodies demanding higher fees for supervision, more co-ordinated attention would seem to be needed to establish standards.'

'We have been trying to evolve a new kind of community-based placement which would not be confined within the boundaries of one particular agency. We are also seeking to involve the voluntary agencies in a closer partnership with the statutory social work services. A multi-faceted placement would offer students the chance to examine opportunities for intervention and use appropriate methods. The placement would be in a specific geographical area and the student would be allocated to a supervisor who might or might not be employed by an established agency. The major role of this supervisor would be to act as a resource person using her knowledge of the locality and her social knowledge and skills in teaching a practice area. This supervisor would be a central person in the students' learning experience although an important function of the role would be to indicate other people in the area who could be significant for the students' total learning. She would help the students to integrate their experience and would liaise with the tutor to design a meaningful experience. The tutor would also be in the role of resource person and through this link the student and supervisor would have general access to the resources of the teaching institution.'

'There is difficulty in distinguishing, in the overall pattern, between the focus of basic course fieldwork and the focus of professional training, bearing in mind that basic course fieldwork is related essentially to the study of social administration and/or sociology.'

'The community work students feel their identity very much more with some kind of political reform in the active promotion of social change rather than with remedial work.'

'To gain fully from fieldwork experience it is essential that there should be theoretical teaching running alongside fieldwork experience.'

'We decided we should have had more modest expectations and the more conventional casework placement has since been used, with the expectation that students would be offered the opportunity wherever feasible to learn about community organisation and development during those placements . . . One recent development has been the use of part of the final placement of some students for promoting their thinking about the needs of particular categories of people in an area and then compiling a register of resources and assessing the need for new services, for example the needs of the mentally handicapped.'

'Our experience was that students could not integrate community work teaching into practice. They found it so far removed from the practice they were experiencing in placements that they could not appreciate its relevance. The students on the early courses tended to be either young and inexperienced or those who had spent a number of years in rather rigid local authority welfare departments. The standard of teaching in fieldwork placements was a great problem. Yet if teaching was to be effective, students had to be able to relate it to practice. The placement situation is gradually improving but remains very difficult. As some social work departments begin to extend their work into the community greater opportunity will be offered for students to be involved.'

'One of the drawbacks of one placement only in community work is that most students became involved in the study and planning phase, but few got through to implementation and evaluation. A lack of a clearly defined theoretical basis for the practice of community work is reflected in the work done in the field.'

'We are experimenting with setting up our own projects, under the supervision of qualified and experienced social workers, who for reasons of family commitments had withdrawn from full-time social work practice. The projects are all based in socially and economically deprived areas and the focus is on helping students to explore the needs of such communities. An attachment to one community throughout the whole first year gives the students the chance to learn about an area in some depth. They undertake surveys, leaflet distribution, and other activities that introduce them to the inhabitants and greatly enrich the learning situation for the student.'

'We are very pleased at the initiative of the students in their community work placements and the way they relate their theory to their practical work. Generally they gain a sensitivity to community needs and the part that community approaches can play as a complement to individual and small group methods of social work. The teaching about community work is not intended to give a comprehensive training in community work but to give students an imaginative awareness of a community approach to social problems.'

'We feel that community work placements have a very important part to play in the training of caseworkers and only regret that the practical problems at present prevent us from carrying our ideas further.'

'Students are provided with typed outlines of the nature and purpose of their community work placements, what to look for and how to make some assessment of the value of the work. Preparation takes a long time and requires careful liaison but the work forms a basis for much useful learning both in practical terms and in relation to on-going seminar work in which basic ideas and principles are clarified.'

'The equivalent of two days a week are allocated to supervised field practice throughout the year. Much of this is undertaken in the Southwark Community Project. Problems include (1) timing of class content in relation to fieldwork and vice versa; (2) difficulty of reconciling the demands and opportunities of field practice with the course time-table, class work and the domestic responsibilities of course members; (3) tendency for field practice to be largely concerned with the establishment of relationships, study, analysis, the creation of appropriate structures, planning and the beginnings of implementation rather than with the later stages of action; (4) tension between carrying real responsibility for a sustained and focused (or limited) piece of field practice as against the attractions of observation and study of a much wider variety of practice. At the end of the course the members, all of whom are seconded by their employing agencies, see many possibilities for community work in the agencies to which they return but wonder how far their agencies will be prepared to pursue the opportunities.'

Some publications on fieldwork placements in community work

Useful material is available in the following publications:

Fieldwork Training for Social Work. Advisory Council on Child Care, Department of Health and Social Security, HMSO 1971.

The Teaching of Fieldwork: Report of the Working Party on Fieldwork. Council for Training in Social Work, Discussion Paper no. 4, 1971 (available from the Central Council for Education and Training in Social Work).

Supervision of Community Work Students, published by the National Council of Social Service, 1969.

Fieldwork Supervision for Community Work Students, NCSS 1970.

Supervision in Community Work Placements, the Report of a Day Conference sponsored by the JUC, March 1972, The Aberdeen Association of Social Service.

Conclusion

This analysis of the replies to a letter of enquiry about the teaching of community work and the list of recent publications on fieldwork show steadily expanding provision for such teaching and practice in existing or new courses. This is still, however, at the pioneer stage with varying aims, tentative experimentation with the range and content of classroom teaching and general concern about the difficulties of raising field teaching to an acceptable standard.

Appendix 4
Detailed content of four community work courses
(See chapter 7, p. 106)

The following are extracts from four prospectuses for 1971–2.

Aberdeen University: Two-year Certificate in Applied Social Studies

Some general principles:

1 It is imperative that students who wish to be employed as professional social workers should have some familiarity with the perspectives and skills associated with community work.
2 The theory and practice of community work should be an integral part of social work training and not merely an addition or an alternative to other parts of a curriculum.
3 The inclusion of community work as part of social work training can be integrated into a two year programme. In such a period it is possible to give sufficient attention to the various levels and contexts of social work practice, whether in casework, community work or residential care. An important feature of teaching community work is that its usefulness and relevance should be compared with other aspects of social work practice and social policy. Such comparisons can be carried out in a relatively unhurried and balanced way in a two-year programme.

Curriculum details:

1 One term and a two-month block community work placement are provided for that aspect of the curriculum which emphasises community work, although it is inevitably also referred to in other courses such as social policy and planning.

a. In the third term at the end of the first year all students attend a course which comes under the general rubric 'Promoters of Change: Conflicts Confronting the Social Worker'. These lectures and seminars are based on the assumption that all professional social workers should have some familiarity with the perspectives and skills associated with community work. They are also intended to provide some preparation for the two-month block community placements which follow. There are three objectives in this introductory course.
   i. to consider the interdependent processes of conflict and change inherent in much community work.
   ii. to consider definitions and examples of community work.
   iii. to look at the various levels of community work paying particular reference to the roles of professional community workers.

b. Students take part in placements in various contexts of community development and community organisation throughout Britain and abroad. These placements are carefully chosen to meet students' needs and interests and to provide a wide cross section of community work experience for all Aberdeen students. Such experiences provide a broad sample for subsequent assessment of the nature of community work and the relevance of present training.

c. In the autumn term at the beginning of the second year students and staff take part in a series of seminars to evaluate the summer placements. This includes a comparison of students' experiences with statements in the literature on community work and a comparison of students' feelings about the different contexts of social work practice and the relationship of community workers to others with social service jobs.

2   Our training is planned to give all students a general preparation for social work but students may place greater emphasis on community work if they wish to do so. Such students may be given further community work placements in the second year. This would be on a concurrent basis and would follow the two-month block placement in the summer. Just as the student who wishes to specialise in psychiatric social work may be given a placement under a PSW in the second year, so the student who develops interest in community work can be placed under a community worker for his final period of fieldwork.

Birmingham Polytechnic: CNAA Four-year Sociology Degree: Community Work option

We particularly draw attention to an almost unique feature in this degree —the training it offers in a growing field of interest in our society: community work. As yet few educational institutions offer such a course, though there is no lack of demand for persons with community work skills. This demand is bound to increase as population expands and as the need for overspill and urban renewal becomes even more urgent and as we grasp the implications of the comparatively recent endeavours of mainly voluntary agencies to bring about a revitalisation of existing centres of population. Changes generated by social and economic factors require, amongst other things, study and control. Social planning is an accepted fact of life today, but increasingly Governments are becoming aware that it can have the effect of reducing the citizen to the status of recipient rather than participant. This is a point that can be elaborated, but suffice it to say that we feel that the community work option will produce a new kind of community worker not concerned primarily with the individual and small group, but with larger social groups of various kinds with various problems of community living. They may be employed as field workers, or in planning or in the administration of the social services (particularly in the enlarged departments of local authorities recommended by the Seebohm Report).

Principles and methods of community work:

Aim: To analyse the motives, aims and methods of community work, and, linked with practical work, to develop in the student the skills of the community worker.

Syllabus

The concept of 'community'—the contribution of sociological theory. Application of the concept with reference to physical planning, redevelopment and revitalisation of existing centres of population.

The meaning of community work. The development of community work— the British tradition; the American tradition; community work in underdeveloped and developing territories. Objectives of community work.

Values and ethics in community work. The concept of morality, moral conduct—the notions of 'right' and 'wrong'. 'Moral' issues and 'social' issues. The concepts of 'rights', 'freedom', 'responsibility', 'authority'. Political and social obligation. Community work and moral issues; the values which underlie intervention. The 'problem' of value judgments in community work.

Methods and techniques in community work. The community worker's roles—guide, enabler, advocate, planner, expert, therapist, catalyst, stimulator. Relationships between agency function and community worker's role. The community worker's tasks—exploration, utilising and building organisations, formulation of policy, implementing plans, evaluation of operation and feedback. The 'tools' of community work—working with and through individuals, groups, organisations, committees, the maintenance of records, publicity and communication. The skills of the community worker: inter-personal skills, group skills, interviewing skills, educational methods—including recruiting and training of voluntary auxiliaries, resource recruitment and management, recording and reporting, public relations techniques. Variation according to agency type and base; public service agencies—personal social service, planning; voluntary agencies— multi-purpose, single-purpose agencies.

Communication in community work: Intra-agency, inter-agency, interpersonal.

The public relations element in community work. The importance of understanding different frames of reference, power structures, significant individuals and groups, informal and formal communication networks.

Task and work methods of other professional groups in related fields— e.g. social caseworkers, social group workers, medical workers, planners, problem solving—their roles in community work.

Dilemmas and problems of community work: inter-organisational coordination and planning; the role of the community worker and his agency in promoting change, in encouraging individuals and groups to articulate needs and press for changes; the differing perceptions of the workers' role—those of the employer, the worker himself, other professional workers, clients. Change and conflict.

Manchester University Department of Adult Education: One-year Diploma in Community Development

1 *Objectives*

The objectives are:

(a) To help postgraduate and post-experience students towards a perspective on community work, an understanding of the context in which it takes place, and a mastery of it as a discipline drawing on education and the other applied social sciences for its conceptual framework;

(b) To provide a setting in which students can identify, analyse and discuss specific issues in community work, and examine the relation between theory and practice;

(c) To familiarise the students with available tools and techniques, including skills of communication, basic analytical and research methods, and the planning and management skills needed for effective community work.

2 *Formal structure and requirements*

Under Faculty regulations entrants to the course may be graduates; or professionally trained teachers or social workers who have at least two years' practical experience in a relevant field.

The programme occupies one academic session, i.e. full-time attendance over three terms.

Candidates are required to satisfy the examiners in three written papers and to submit a dissertation of about 15,000 words on an approved subject in the area of community work.

3 *Outline of programme*

The programme comprises lectures, seminars, structured and un-structured group sessions, practical exercises and visits to centres, community projects and locations of professional relevance to individual students' needs. This year, as an experiment, it also includes a short residential course on group methods of learning.

Individual and group tutorials occupy about 100 hours of programme time.

Course provision is centred on the examinable subjects, namely:

(a) *Principles of community development and community organisation,* including analysis of the two action systems, their origins and practice in the U.K. situation;

(b) *Communication,* in the context of community work, including consideration of mass media and the specific problems of communication in local authority and neighbourhood settings, and in planning and community programmes.

(c) *Community action:* a study of the incidence and meaning of community initiatives occurring outside formal bureaucrati c structures, whether in opposition to these, or to supplement their work.

Additional courses are offered to widen the student's conceptual framework or introduce him to practical skills and techniques. Examples of optional courses are:

Concepts in social science, politics and economics
Lecturing and discussion techniques
Adult learning and group relations
Audio-visual aids
The use of broadcasting and television
Statistical methods and applications
Introduction to research techniques
Organisation and administration
Training and evaluation

York University: One-year Diploma in Community Work

Course content:
All students will undertake four courses, i.e.

Community work theory
Community work practice
Dissertation
One option

For those without a background in sociology, there is a course in Introduction to Sociology. Students without previous knowledge of social administration will take the course followed by Diploma in Social Administration students.
Other options are available by agreement with staff at the beginning of the year.

Fieldwork

Fieldwork will consist of:
1.   An on-going placement to begin as soon as possible in the autumn term and to continue until Easter. This is expected to occupy two days a week, and arrangements will be worked out with students individually in the first weeks of term. An outline will be given of on-going activities in York and opportunities will be available also in Leeds.
2.   A number of visits of observation and group projects.
3.   A short observation placement of three weeks.
4.   A six-week summer placement.

Community work theory

First term
1.   Theories of community. Definitions. The validity of the 'community study' approach. Community in an urban setting. The neighbourhood concept, etc.
2.   Approaches to community work. Definitions. A critical study of books on community work. (See appropriate reading list.) Study and action models. Applicability of approaches to contemporary British setting.
3.   Social structure of modern Britain. Aspects of class, education, social

institutions, political framework, values and culture, etc., and their relevance to community work.

Second and third terms
4. Theories of social change.
5. Power structures and pressure group politics.
6. Sociology of social problems.
7. Leadership and group dynamics.
8. Methods of social research.

Community work practice

First term
1. Background to community work. Historical perspective. Development of contemporary practice settings. Emergence of social action strategies.
2. Community work settings. Local authority social services departments, councils of social service, new communities, community relations, community development projects, neighbourhood work, youth and community work, social planning.
Second and third terms
3. Case studies:
   a. differing practice settings
   b. community work skills.
4. Values in community work.
5. Relationships with other professions.

References

ADENEY, M. (1970) 'A say in the way they live', *Guardian*, 7 August.

ALINSKY, S. (1969) *Reveille for Radicals*, New York, Random House.

ALINSKY, S. (1970) *The Professional Radical*, New York, Harper & Row.

ARMSTRONG, R. (1972) 'Towards the study of community action', *Adult Education*, vol. 45, no. 1.

AVES, G. M. (chairman) (1969) *The Voluntary Worker in the Social Services* (National Council of Social Service and National Institute for Social Work Training), Allen & Unwin.

BARR, A. (1971) 'A neighbourhood project in Birmingham' (duplicated).

BATTEN, T. R. (1967) *The Non-directive Approach in Group and Community Work*, Oxford University Press.

BENNINGTON, J. (1971) 'Community development', *Municipal and Public Service Journal*, 22, 29 January.

BION, W. R. (1961) *Experiences in Groups, and other papers*, Tavistock Publications.

BRADSHAW, J. R. (1970) 'Welfare rights: a strategy of social action' (duplicated).

BRIGGS, A. (chairman) (1972) *Report of the Committee on Nursing*, HMSO.

BRYANT, R. (1972) 'Community action', *British Journal of Social Work*, vol. 2, no. 2.

CENTRAL HOUSING ADVISORY COMMITTEE (1967) *The Needs of New Communities*, HMSO.

COUNCIL FOR THE EDUCATION AND TRAINING OF HEALTH VISITORS (1970) Evidence to the Committee on Nursing.

CLOWARD, R. A. and PIVEN, F. F. (1969) 'The professional bureaucracies: benefit systems as influence systems' in R. M. Kramer and H. Specht (eds), *Readings in Community Organization Practice*, Prentice-Hall.

COHEN, N. (1971) review of *Community Work and Social Change*, in *International Social Work*, vol. 14, no. 2.

DEPARTMENT OF THE ENVIRONMENT (1972) *Town and Country Planning Act*, 1971. Part II: *Development Plan Proposals: Publicity and Public Participation*, Joint Circular 52/72 and 104/72 (Welsh Office), HMSO.

DEPARTMENT OF HEALTH AND SOCIAL SECURITY (1970) *National Health Service: the Future Structure of the N.H.S.*, HMSO.

DEPARTMENT OF HEALTH AND SOCIAL SECURITY (1972) *National Health Service Reorganization: England*, HMSO.

DEPARTMENT OF LOCAL GOVERNMENT (1970) *Reform of Local Government in England*, HMSO.

DONNISON, D. V. and CHAPMAN, V. (1965) *Social Policy and Administration*, Allen & Unwin.

DUNHAM, A. (1970) *The New Community Organisation*, New York, Crowell.

GHAZZALI, A. (1972) 'A survey of advertised posts for community workers in public and voluntary services' (duplicated, Department of Adult Education, Manchester University; available from the Gulbenkian Foundation, £1).

GOETSCHIUS, G. (1969) *Working with Community Groups*, Routledge & Kegan Paul.

GULBENKIAN FOUNDATION (1968) *Community Work and Social Change*, Longmans.

GURIN, A. (1970) *Community Organisation Curriculum in Graduate Social Work Education*, New York, Council on Social Work Education.

HALSEY, A. H. (ed.) (1972) *Educational Priority*, vol. 1: *EPA Problems and Policies*, HMSO.

HARINGEY FAMILY ADVICE CENTRE (1970) 'First thoughts on participation' (unpublished paper).

HILL, M. J. and ISSACHAROFF, R. (1971) *Community Action and Race Relations*, Oxford University Press.

HINDESS, B. (1971) *The Decline of Working-class Politics*, MacGibbon & Kee.

HISCOX, J. (1972) 'Wolverhampton Young Volunteer Force foundation' (duplicated).

HODGE, P. (1970) 'The future of community development' in W. Robson and B. Crick (eds), *The Future of the Social Services*, Penguin.

HOLMAN, R. (1968) 'Client power', *New Society*, 31 October.

HOLMAN, R. (1972a) *Power for the Powerless: The Role of Community Action*, Community and Race Relations Unit of the British Council of Churches.

HOLMAN, R. (1972b) 'Students and community action', *Universities Quarterly*, vol. 26, no. 2.

INKELES, A. (1966) *What is Sociology?*, Prentice-Hall.

JAMES, LORD (chairman) (1971) *Teacher Education and Training*, HMSO.

JERMAN, B. (1971) *Do Something! A Guide to Self-help Organizations*, Garnstone Press.

KILBRANDON, LORD (chairman) (1964) *Children and Young Persons (Scotland)*, HMSO.

LAPPING, A. (ed.) (1970) *Community Action*, Fabian tract no. 400.

MARRIS, P. and REIN, M. (1967) *Dilemmas of Social Reform*, Routledge & Kegan Paul.

MILSON, F. (1972) 'The teacher as community worker' (duplicated, available from Westhill College of Education, Birmingham).

MITTON, R. and MORRISON, E. (1972) *A Community Project in Notting Dale*, Allen Lane, the Penguin Press.

MOORHOUSE, G. (1970) 'The royal rotten borough', *Guardian*, 24 September.

MUCHNICK, D. (1970) *Urban Renewal in Liverpool*, Bell.

NANDY, D. (1970) 'The urban crisis' (unpublished paper).

NATIONAL COUNCIL OF SOCIAL SERVICE (1969) Report of the review committee.

PLOWDEN, LADY (chairman) (1967) *Children and their Primary Schools* (Central Advisory Council for Education), HMSO.

POPPLESTONE, G. (1972) 'Collective action among private tenants', *British Journal of Social Work*, vol. 2, no. 3.

POWER, A. (1970) 'Development of the Housing Action Group, May 1969—May 1970' (duplicated).

POWER, A. (1972) *I Woke Up This Morning*, Community and Race Relations Unit of the British Council of Churches.

REDCLIFFE-MAUD, LORD (chairman) (1969) *Report of the Royal Commission on Local Government in England*, HMSO.

ROYAL TOWN PLANNING INSTITUTE (1971) Examinations Handbook.

RUSSELL, SIR LIONEL (chairman) (1973) *Adult Education: A Plan for Development*, HMSO.

SEEBOHM, LORD (chairman) (1968) *Report of the Committee on Local Authority and Allied Personal Social Services*, HMSO.

SKEFFINGTON, A. M. (chairman) (1969) *People and Planning* (Committee on Public Participation in Planning), HMSO.

SMITH, C. S. and ANDERSON, B. (1972) 'Political participation through community action' in G. Parry (ed.), *Participation in Politics*, Manchester University Press.

SMITH, K. G. M. (1972) 'Report and assessment of the squatting campaign in Redbridge' (duplicated).

STUART, M. (1971) 'Housing officers keep quiet', *Guardian*, 6 November.

THOMPSON, E. P. (1970) 'Report on Lord Radcliffe', *New Society*, 30 April, pp. 737–8.

TODD, LORD (chairman) (1968) *Report of the Royal Commission on Medical Education* HMSO.

TUGENDHAT, C. (1971) *The Multinationals*, Eyre & Spottiswoode.

UNITED NATIONS (1971) *Popular Participation in Development: Emerging Trends in Community Development*.

WARREN, R. (1964) *Patterns of Community Action*, Waltham, Mass., Brandeis University Papers in Social Welfare, no. 4.

WEBER, M. (1964) *Theory of Social and Economic Organization*, Collier-Macmillan.

WILSON, G. (1970) 'Misery of a forgotten million', *Guardian*, 11 November.

YOUTH SERVICE DEVELOPMENT COUNCIL (1969) *Youth and Community Work in the 70s*, HMSO.

ZALD, M. N. (1966) 'Organizations as polities: an analysis of community organization agencies', *Social Work* (New York), vol. 11, no. 4.